CENTRAL LIBRARY

OCT - 1996

D0202077

FASCINATING COMMENTS
FROM LITERATURE AND EDUCATION
TO ACTIVISM AND ENTERTAINMENT
BY NOTED LATINO AMERICANS:

"We will consider our jobs done when every one of our people recognizes his sense of personal dignity and pride in his history, his culture, and his race." —Luis Valdez

"I was born gifted. I can speak of my gifts with little or no modesty, but with tremendous gratitude, precisely because they are gifts, and not things which I created, or actions about which I might be proud." —Joan Baez

"When I first came to Miami [in 1960], you'd see signs like 'No Children, No Pets, No Cubans.' We were a major threat." —Gloria Estefan

"People think of the Latino population here as recently arrived. But the oldest neighborhoods in town are the Mexican neighborhoods—because it used to be Mexico." —Gregory Nava, filmmaker, *Mi Familia*

"My upbringing taught me that cultures are not isolated, and perish when deprived of contact with what is different and challenging." —Carlos Fuentes

THE FIRE IN OUR SOULS

Rosie Gonzalez is actively involved in the charitable organizations Casa de Los Niños in Tucson, Arizona, and Hospice-by-the-Bay in San Francisco. She has taught English as a Second Language to children and battered women.

THE
FIRE IN OUR SOULS

Quotations of Wisdom and Inspiration by
Latino Americans

Rosie Gonzalez

ANOTHER WORK BY
AFFINITY COMMUNICATIONS CORPORATION

A PLUME BOOK

PLUME
Published by the Penguin Group
Penguin Books USA Inc., 375 Hudson Street, New York, New York 10014, U.S.A.
Penguin Books Ltd, 27 Wrights Lane, London W8 5TZ, England
Penguin Books Australia Ltd, Ringwood, Victoria, Australia
Penguin Books Canada Ltd, 10 Alcorn Avenue, Toronto, Ontario, Canada M4V 3B2
Penguin Books (N.Z.) Ltd, 182-190 Wairau Road, Auckland 10, New Zealand

Penguin Books Ltd, Registered Offices: Harmondsworth, Middlesex, England

First published by Plume, an imprint of Dutton Signet,
a division of Penguin Books USA Inc.

First Printing, October, 1996
10 9 8 7 6 5 4 3 2 1

Copyright © Affinity Communications Corporation, 1996
All rights reserved

ACKNOWLEDGMENTS
Cover photographs: Top (l-r): UPI/Corbis-Bettmann, UPI/Corbis-Bettmann,
Reuters/Corbis-Bettmann, UPI/Corbis-Bettmann, Michael Ferguson/Globe
Photos, Inc. Bottom (l-r): © Jane Shirek/Outline, Theodore Wood/Globe Photos,
Inc., John Barrett/Globe Photos, Inc., Sylvia Norris/Globe Photos, Inc., © Miriam
Berkley

 REGISTERED TRADEMARK—MARCA REGISTRADA

LIBRARY OF CONGRESS CATALOGING-IN-PUBLICATION DATA: TK
The fire in our souls : quotations of wisdom and inspiration by Latino-
    Americans / [compiled by] Rosie Gonzalez.
        p.   cm.
    ISBN 0-452-27684-5
    1. Hispanic Americans—Quotations.   I. Gonzalez, Rosie.
PN6084.H47F57   1996
081'.08968—dc20
                                                                96-20579
                                                                CIP

Printed in the United States of America
Set in ITC Century Light and Benguiat
Designed by Eve L. Kirch

Without limiting the rights under copyright reserved above, no part of this publi-
cation may be reproduced, stored in or introduced into a retrieval system, or
transmitted, in any form, or by any means (electronic, mechanical, photocopy-
ing, recording, or otherwise), without the prior written permission of both the
copyright owner and the above publisher of this book.

BOOKS ARE AVAILABLE AT QUANTITY DISCOUNTS WHEN USED TO PROMOTE PRODUCTS
OR SERVICES. FOR INFORMATION PLEASE WRITE TO PREMIUM MARKETING DIVISION,
PENGUIN BOOKS USA INC., 375 HUDSON STREET, NEW YORK, NY 10014.

CONTENTS

ACKNOWLEDGMENTS

One person is not capable of pulling together a resource such as this book of quotations. Maybe after the book has existed a number of years, like *Bartlett's Familiar Quotations*, the process will become more or less automatic: update, add here and there . . . and it's finished. But this first effort would not have happened without the intense contributions of many people, especially the compiler, Laraine Crampton. Chief among them is José Luis Sedano, whose immediate responsiveness and determined generosity with his time, amazing telephone list, imagination, and energy renewed the project when it seemed impossible to complete. And if Karen Grube had not initiated the book and provided the initial (and substantial) labor to get it off the ground, we might still be waiting for it to happen.

Those who assisted by sending in or E-mailing selections include Tom McAlpine from Costa Rica; Rubén Martínez, who imperiled his own deadlines and travel schedule; Gustavo LeClerc, for whom sacrificing valuable personal time for a larger project seems to be second nature; Naomi Quiñonez, who trekked to the library on the same Saturday that she completed her dissertation to be sure material and encouragement arrived on time; and Jaime Oaxaca, whose impassioned certainty that this book must serve its purpose well has been a strong point of inspiration. The staff at the East Los Angeles County Library's Chicano Research Center were graciously helpful and most supportive to several of us (on at least one occasion, to several of us at once!), and Richard Chabran at UCLA's Chicano Resource Center did his best to bring this work to the attention of librarians on the Internet and opened the center to us.

There are others who deserve mention, and more who will deserve greater mention. Don't make the mistake of thinking the compiler wrote this book: the people who spoke or wrote or created the lines are the ones to look at, and the kind souls who helped to gather the quotes from out of sometimes very resistant thin air deserve the real credit.

FOREWORD

I am often asked to participate in many worthwhile programs designed to foster awareness of the tremendous contributions Latinos have made to the American way of life. Unfortunately, I'm not always able to become as involved as I would like to be. When I was first approached to write the foreword to *The Fire in Our Souls*, I was quite intrigued. Because of the lasting impact books have, this was a tremendous opportunity to become involved in a project that could touch thousands of lives for years to come. However, I was a bit skeptical. Would the book really articulate the passionate voices of Latinos? Would it help break negative stereotypes? Would it appeal to and inspire non-Latinos as well as Latinos? In fact, this book does all that, and more. I am honored to be associated with *The Fire in Our Souls* and hope that you gain as much insight into the Latino culture and way of life as the people quoted had hopefully intended with their words.

—EDWARD JAMES OLMOS

INTRODUCTION

I am delighted to introduce *The Fire in Our Souls*.

Cultural literacy should be part of everyone's body of knowledge. However, the cultural literacy establishment of the United States has for the most part been oblivious to the collective or individual accomplishments of Latinos in America. I welcome this opportunity to underscore the many contributions of Latinos whose actions speak louder than words, yet whose eloquence often falls on deaf ears.

Latinos speak to us in the clearest voice America understands: hard work. Thanks in part to the labor of all those hardworking recent arrivals from Latin America, it costs less to live in the United States than in any other industrialized country in the world. Although today they pick crops, cook food, and wash dishes, tomorrow they will be naturalized citizens whose children might someday grow up to be the president of the United States. Let us not forget that the largest number of Congressional Medals of Honor awarded in the history of the U.S. armed forces—

thirty-eight—were presented to Mexican-Americans and Puerto Ricans.

The United States, with a population of approximately twenty-six million Americans of Latin descent, is now the fifth-largest Latin American country in the world. Small business is the backbone of American strength, but few people realize how many Latino-owned small businesses exist. There are more than 115,000 in Los Angeles County alone, and comparable numbers in Miami, Chicago, New York, and the Southwest.

Nevertheless, we are largely absent from English-language network television, network news, PBS, CNN, talk shows, theater, radio, print media, and feature films. Latinos constitute 10 percent of the population and earn more than $200 billion annually, yet our children grow up without seeing positive images of themselves on television. By the year 2040, Hispanic Americans will be the largest group of Americans, including 50 percent of the population of California. In short, Latinos will play an indispensable part in the future of the United States.

Our influences are not, of course, exclusively North American writers, poets, businesspeople, scientists, and educators. Rigoberta Menchú, Pablo Neruda, Octavio Paz, Alfonso García Robles, and Dr. Mario Molina are all *American* Nobel Prize laureates, and they were born in Guatemala, Chile, and Mexico, respectively. This is just a gentle reminder that you don't have to be born a Connecticut Yankee to be an American.

It is my hope that *The Fire in Our Souls* will be a sourcebook that our youth, parents, adults, and educators can use to begin to hear the articulate voices of our contemporary leadership. While this book is but one step in correcting past omissions, it allows the reader to hear the

Introduction

voice of reason, smile at the humor, and appreciate the wisdom of so many Latino Americans. I hope that *The Fire in Our Souls* will act as a reminder that Latinos are and have always been active contributors to life in the United States of America.

—JOSÉ LUIS SEDANO, cofounder and board member of the National Hispanic Media Coalition

ACTING/ACTORS

There's a whole new breed.... They are just well trained actors who just happen to be Hispanic. We're just playing people and not playing the results of people, especially negative people.
          —ELIZABETH PEÑA, actress
          Los Angeles Herald Examiner, July 6, 1987

I came to be an actor. I didn't come here to be a stereotype. So I always looked for the opportunity to do something that was challenging. I never wanted to take the easy route.

          —RAÚL JULIA, actor
          Hispanic Business, July 1992

I started as a classical actor at the Old Globe when I was seventeen. I feel an artist must create as he must breathe: without one or the other, he has neither life nor soul.
          —RICK NAJERA, comedian

I have been stubborn in refusing to do certain types of roles that feed into that distortion, that feed into that horrible misrepresentation—the drug dealer of the month, that kind of garbage. I don't know if I wouldn't have done those roles if I had been starving, but it never quite came to it.

—HECTOR ELIZONDO, actor
Los Angeles Times, February 9, 1983

The challenge is to keep moving and learning, never to settle for any of the same until you're rotting in your own comfort.

—RAÚL JULIA, actor
Hispanic Business, July 1992

It can be a cruel industry. It takes no prisoners. You develop a very hard shell or you're out. . . . All actors have to be stubborn or they'd never find work. Stubbornness and persistence is what got me where I am today.

—ANDY GARCÍA, actor
Redbook, January 1993

To have creative choice as an actor, where you can choose from the very few well-written things every year, is a fortunate position to be in.

—ANDY GARCÍA, actor
Rising Voices: Profiles in Leadership

Acting/Actors

You hear people say so-and-so is "one of the great black actors," or he's "a great Latino actor." But they don't say about Dustin [Hoffman], "He's one of the great Jewish actors." We're all just actors.

—ANDY GARCÍA, actor
Redbook, January 1993

I want to be an actor. Period. They don't call Robert De Niro and Al Pacino famous Italian actors.

—ESAI MORALES, actor
Hispanic Hollywood

I'll be damned if they call me a Latin actor. Nobody calls Sinatra an Italian singer. I'm an actor, period. . . . I've gotten all these roles on my own. Just think how many I would have gotten if my name was not Elizondo.

—HECTOR ELIZONDO, actor
Hispanic Hollywood

Do I feel lucky? No, I don't feel lucky. Luck would have been a limo picking me up when I arrived in L.A. in 1978, or sitting next to a casting agent on the plane, who would have put me in his next movie. No, I don't feel lucky. I have too many war wounds.

—ANDY GARCÍA, actor
Redbook, January 1993

Cyrano was such an important step in my career, such a turning point. I had borrowed money when I was 34 years old and produced it on Broadway, starring myself. Four years later, there I was making a movie of [it].
—José Ferrer, actor, director
Dramalogue, October 8, 1987

I tend to get possessed by things I do. If I'm not passionate about something, I don't feel I can act the role out. I'd rather not work if I don't have some emotional connection to the role.
—Andy García, actor
Rising Voices: Profiles in Leadership

ACTIVISM

I realized one day that as a teacher I couldn't do anything for the kids who came to school barefoot and hungry.

> —DOLORES HUERTA, activist
> "Dolores Huerta Talks About Republicans,
> César, Children and Her Home Town,"
> *Regeneracion*, vol. 2, no. 4, 1975

One of the reasons why we are so insecure is that we really do not have that many models. WE are just solidifying. So we don't have enough to choose models from. We are all pioneers. And we are all fumbling, the best and the worst. It will take another seventy-five years before someone really solidifies the movement.

> —ESTELA PORTILLO TRAMBLEY, author

Concentration is inspiration. You must be completely overtaken by your work and your subject. Only then do all your influences and experience come up to the surface.
    —CÉSAR CHÁVEZ, activist
      Roots of Greatness: The 1995 Mexican-American Historical Calendar

We will win in the end. We learned many years ago that the rich may have the money, but the poor have the time.
    —CÉSAR CHÁVEZ, activist
      Newsweek, September 22, 1975

I can do my terrorist activities now by staying at home and writing. I have the power to make people think in a different way. It's a different way of defining power, and it is something that I don't want to abuse or lose. I want to help my community.
    —SANDRA CISNEROS, author
      quoted by Mary B. W. Tabor in volume 1 of *Hispanic Literature Criticism*

¡Viva la huelga [Long live the strike]!
    —CÉSAR CHÁVEZ, activist
      slogan of the United Farm Workers

We don't have a choice but to use economic measures. These entities [media and corporations] won't change their actions because they *like us* and want to do *what's best* for the community. They will only act when it hurts their pocketbooks.
    —ALEX NOGALES, National Hispanic Media Coalition
      Hispanic Business, October 1995

You must understand—I must make you understand—that our membership and the hopes and inspirations of the hundreds of thousands of the poor and dispossessed that have been raised on our account are above all, human beings, no better, no worse, than any other cross section of human society; we are not saints because we are poor but by the same measure neither are we immoral. We are men and women who have suffered and endured much and not only because of our abject poverty but because we have been kept poor. The colors of our skins, the languages of our cultural and native origins, the lack of formal education, the exclusion from the democratic process, the numbers of our slain in recent wars—all these burdens generation after generation have sought to demoralize us, to break our human spirit. But God knows that we are men.

> —Cέsar Chávez, activist
> from a letter to E. L. Barr, Jr., president of the
> California Grape and Tree Fruit League

The old who know him will die. Younger generations will name public schools after César Chávez. The boxer Julio Cesar Chavez will retire. The young will turn blithely away from the past, as only the young dare to do. César Chávez will be forgotten in the city. But he belongs forever in California, in ways deeper than memory. He brought from Mexico a spirit of resilience; he planted a challenge on the land. He stood under an unforgiving sun. The cloudless sky does not forget such people.

> —Richard Rodriguez, author
> *Los Angeles Times*, May 2, 1993

Wherever there are Mexican people, wherever there are farmworkers, our movement is spreading like flames across a dry plain. . . . The time has come for the liberation of the poor farmworker. History is on our side. May the strike go on! ¡Que viva la cause!

—CÉSAR CHÁVEZ, activist
Roots of Greatness

Pachucos are becoming folk heroes because they were rebels. And sensitive people need to understand rebellion because they know it is not created in a vacuum. There's always a reason for rebellion.

—RUBÉN SALAZAR, journalist
Los Angeles Times, July 17, 1970

You have to learn to laugh at yourself and not take yourself so seriously. People have often asked, "Do you really think that you're going to end the war in Central America with what you're doing?" And they're right, it would be ridiculous to think that. But at the same time, if there ever is peace in Central America, I can look back and say that maybe by adding my little grain of sand to the situation, I had something to do with it.

—FATHER LUIS OLIVARES, pastor
LA Weekly, September 6–12, 1991

The fight is never about grapes or lettuce. It is always about people.

—CÉSAR CHÁVEZ, activist
Rising Voices: Profiles in Leadership

ART/ARTISTS

Architects, artists and designers must search for a more democratic way of designing. We must listen to the voices of our communities as expressed in their transformation and appropriation of already existing spaces and structures because these are visible memory and evidence of those who have been treated as invisible people.

—ALLESSANDRA MOCTEZUMA, architect
L.A. Architect: The Dialog Begins

[Commenting on the workings of the publishing industry:] ... and there's this pecking order ... I find it offensive. . . . It's everything that I don't believe art is about. Art is about being a little wild, taking risks, not necessarily getting approval from somebody; it's the disapproval.

—DAGOBERTO GILB, author
Los Angeles Times Magazine,
November 12, 1995

There are no exact rules, even by experts who absorb their lives with the history and knowledge of art, as to what is "good art." Opinions and beliefs about art keep changing with the time and course of history. Nothing remains stable but that art always remains. It is seen in its own context, time and circumstances. It cannot be measured scientifically—but then isn't that also part and parcel of its beauty and mystery?

—MAUREEN LEON ACOSTA, director
Expresiones Hispanas 88/89

An image is a bridge between evoked emotion and conscious knowledge; words are the cables that hold up the bridge. Images are more direct, more immediate than words, and closer to the unconscious. Picture language precedes thinking in words; the metaphorical mind precedes analytical consciousness.

—GLORIA ANZALDÚA, author
Borderlands/La Frontera: The New Mestiza

I feel that one of the responsibilities of the arts leaders is to encourage and be firm and determine to present what they, as leaders, feel is true art and not be led mainly by trends and sometimes media-fabricated publicity.

—MARTA ISTOMIN, artistic director
Washingtonian, December 1987

Basically, I view artists as a kind of filter, with a sensitive radar that captures what is happening in our society. We . . . are part of the culture of our time, and we act as visual historians and critics, too, because art has a social function. Any society that doesn't value art remains at the primitive, animal level. Art touches the soul of a culture.

> —HUMBERTO CALZADA, artist
> *Barrios and Borderlands*

[Art is also] the culture of those people without power, and you find that in the street, where the people use it to empower themselves.

> —GUSTAVO LECLERC, architect, artist
> "Stylemakers," *L.A. Style*, 1994

The universality of the artist's message is linked with the values of the society from which the ideas spring, though the artist may not necessarily agree with the values expressed.

> —FELIX ANGEL, architect, painter
> *Expresiones Hispanas 88/89*

There exists a pervasive myth, contrary to ample and increasing evidence, that hardly any *"really"* serious art emerges out of Southern California. This myth of creative aridity persists despite the intimate courtship of countless major artists who have been fascinated by the vicissitudes of this enigmatic city, painting it, writing about it, living here off-and-on or permanently.

> —JOHN RECHY, author
> from the preface to *The Southern California Anthology 1984*

It is true that in Cuba and Puerto Rico certain themes and ideas have held interest for writers and artists: religion and magic (be it Catholic or African), national identity and violent struggle, music, the patriarchal family, the surreal quality of the Caribbean environment, and a certain baroque spirit that is reflected in everything from architecture to language. But if many artists utilize these elements or themes, they often do so in ways that are not blatantly obvious. Others choose not to make use of them at all or deal with them on levels that are so subliminal that it becomes impossible to come to any definite conclusions.

—GIULIO V. BLANC, art historian
Expresiones Hispanas 88/89

Western cultures behave differently toward works of art than do tribal cultures. The "sacrifices" Western cultures make are in housing their art works in the best structures designed by the best architects; and in servicing them with insurance, guards to protect them, conservators to maintain them, specialists to mount and display them, and the educated and upper classes to "view" them. Tribal cultures keep art works in honored and sacred places in the home and elsewhere. They attend them by making sacrifices of blood (goat or chicken), libations of wine. They bathe, feed, and clothe them.

—GLORIA ANZALDÚA, author
"Tlilli, Tlapalli: The Path of the Red and Black Ink"

You can't go outside of yourself to create, and if the art created is good art, it will speak to all humanity.

—PABLO FIGUEROA, filmmaker
Portraits

Art is an enduring phenomenon of human existence, a search for new avenues of expression and communication. . . . Fine art created by Hispanic artists stands up to the highest criteria of what is quality in "American Art." This art is no longer to be considered a subculture art that can be ignored but rather a valuable contribution that is part of the fabric of cultural wealth that makes up this nation.

—MAUREEN LEON ACOSTA, director
Expresiones Hispanas 88/89

Chicano artists are in a unique position in that they are part of a sequence of interconnected events extending backward in time to before the arrival of the Europeans. This "retro-telescopic" vision compels them to regard the past and present as an organic whole: yesterday is as dear and palpable as today.

—MIGUEL DOMÍNGUEZ, Ph.D., writer, educator

Art is a reflection of life mirrored through the vision of its creator and the witness to that creation. It is a private dialogue between artist and viewer. Each artist contributes their individual perceptions stemming from personal life circumstances, social, historical and political contexts and religious and cultural influences. This unlimited pathway to understanding may be clear or confused, but it is always a search for a new awareness of reality. Art is a nonverbal, often universal, personal communication to those lucky enough to be open to it. This visual experience can evoke the full gamut of emotions from love, passion and exuberance to hatred and profound grief.

—MAUREEN LEON ACOSTA, director
Expresiones Hispanas 88/89

Like artists from other cultural groups around the world, the Hispanic artist belongs to both his own heritage and that of Marshall McLuhan's "global village." While it is natural that an artist's roots and personal experience (vis-à-vis the rest of the world) are important, just as significant are his creative individuality and his relation to the non-Hispanic world in general, and the community of artists which knows no national or temporal boundaries, in particular.

—GIULIO V. BLANC, art historian
Expresiones Hispanas 88/89

I don't want to be just a visual artist, I want to communicate and I want to communicate about issues that I feel are very important to me, and issues that I think are very important for other people that I feel close to.

That means the whole community out there, the whole Chicano community, and by extension the Hispanic community as well, but it also applies to everybody, and so I deal with social issues in a lot of the work.

—LUIS JIMENEZ, artist
The Hispanic Reporter, September 1994

Being a minority that has suffered discrimination and frequently forced assimilation in the 19th and 20th centuries, the Chicano message is frequently one that demands an identity that is separate. The iconography and palette of Chicano art or art created by Chicano artists, therefore, is often affected by socio-political concerns, cultural awareness and deeply rooted artistic dictates.

—MIGUEL DOMÍNGUEZ, Ph.D., writer, educator

Art/Artists

My commitment is to have my nation free ... not as a
political fanatic but as a human rights visionary. As an
artist I can't avoid presenting some of my work as a narrator of things that are happening today in Puerto Rico.
                    —DENNIS MARIO RIVERA, artist
                    Hispanic, January/February 1995

BILINGUALISM

The success of bilingual artists is just a further manifestation of our . . . integration into the American way of life. It's been happening for hundreds of years. This is just another phase.

> —Tony Sabournin, Latin music authority
> *Hispanic*, December 1992

We would meet with administrators, counselors, teachers, parents and anyone else willing to listen to tell them that maybe Chicanos and Hispanics are not your average father, mother, two-point-three children and a dog and a cat and a white fence families; that they bring a beautiful language and a unique culture with them; that we shouldn't try to kill it off, but instead that we should look for these qualities and nurture them while we teach English.

> —Mari-Luci Jaramillo, educator, diplomat
> *Notable Hispanic American Women*

Being bilingual and bicultural is an asset. It is having *twice* as much as most folks. How fortunate can Latinas be? . . . Latinas can have the best of both worlds as well as a choice of who to be.

—BETTINA R. FLORES, author
Chiquita's Cocoon

English-only laws are a throwback to the days when teachers paddled students or washed out their mouths with soap for the crime of speaking Spanish.

—ROBERTO RODRIGUEZ, filmmaker,
and PATRISIA GONZALES, author *Latino Spectrum*

I have a dream. It is to see the realization of social change in this country in the area of accepting the language and culture of others; in the ability to let children make use of their native languages as a skill, and not to destroy this skill. We should want to make all children bilingual when their mother tongue is other than English— whether it is Spanish, Indian, Chinese, or Swahili. We shouldn't try to set up one culture as the one and only one. We should erase the aversion to nonconformity.

—LUPE ANGUIANO, educator
Famous Mexican-Americans

CHURCH

There were times when I thought [Father Luis] Olivares to be something of a demagogue, a romantic revolutionary prone to twist the truth for political ends. At the same time, I wanted to believe in his version of the Gospel, that the words could lead to action, that action could change our lives.

—RUBÉN MARTÍNEZ, journalist
LA Weekly, April 2–8, 1993

What sense does it make to go to Mass on Sunday and reach out for spiritual help, and instead get sermons about the wickedness of your cause? That only drives one to question and to despair.

—CÉSAR CHÁVEZ, activist
"The Mexican-American and the Church"

Church

We like to tout that there are 6 million evangelicos in the U.S. But when we look closely at the research and count the number of Latino congregations and make projections on their size, we only come up with one-and-a-half million. Our question is "Where are the other four-and-a-half million?" Our studies show that many of them are in Anglo churches.

—LUIS MADRIGAL, executive director
Christianity Today, February 6, 1995

Many of our churches are stuck in the nineteenth century when we're already about to enter the twenty-first.

—EDITH LaFONTAINE, editor
Christianity Today, February 6, 1995

If pastors don't learn English, they will be out of a job or kill the church. It's incorrect to say that church has to become bilingual-bicultural. It already is.

—LUIS MADRIGAL, executive director
Christianity Today, February 6, 1995

People look at what we do and ask if we are solving the problems of the parish—if we are changing the poor's and the undocumented's condition in life. I admit that we are not. But I lay great store in the power of symbol to change things. I think that our statement is strong enough to change attitudes.

—FATHER LUIS OLIVARES, pastor
LA Weekly, April 2–8, 1993

Finally, in a nutshell, what do we want the Church to do? We don't ask for more cathedrals. We don't ask for bigger churches or fine gifts. We ask for its presence with us, beside us, as Christ among us. We ask the Church to sacrifice with the people for social change, for justice, and for love of brother. We don't ask for words. We ask for deeds. We don't ask for paternalism. We ask for servanthood.

        —CÉSAR CHÁVEZ, activist
        "The Mexican-American and the Church"

Too many of our priests see the danger of what Communism represents to the Catholic Church. And that's all they think about. This is a mistake that the bishops of Central America are making. I think that this attitude demonstrates a lack of faith and lack of trying to live out the Gospel, one of which is "Love your enemy," or "Do good to those who persecute you."

        —FATHER LUIS OLIVARES, pastor
        El Popo, Spring 1988

The religious imagination is part of the antidote to the Hispanic exodus. If Hispanics are finding a home in other churches, then, ironically, the reason may be that they have been more successful at capturing the Hispanic Catholic imagination than the Catholic Church has. . . . The Hispanic exodus ought to alarm the church not because other churches are stealing their flock but, rather, that the Catholic religious imagination may be dimming.

        —ALEX GARCÍA-RIVERA, pastor
        U.S. Catholic, July 1994

Church

According to the Catholic Church, you can only get to heaven by being good; that is, by not sinning. The problem is that to the Catholic Church almost *everything* is a sin. Even newborn infants are born with original sin and have to be saved through baptism.

—BETTINA R. FLORES, author
Chiquita's Cocoon

The Church has traditionally exercised control through suppression, with a perfect example being the religious life itself. Since "money is evil," you take a vow of poverty and suppress your desire for money. Since "power is evil," you take a vow of obedience and make yourself subject to someone else's authority. Since "sex is evil," you take a vow of chastity in which you totally deny yourself a gift that God created and that is beautiful and good.

—FATHER LUIS OLIVARES, pastor
LA Weekly, September 6–12, 1991

The priest always held First Communion during mid-spring. I'll always remember that day in my life. . . . I hadn't been able to sleep the night before, trying to remember all of my sins, and worse yet, trying to arrive at an exact number. Furthermore, since Mother had placed a picture of hell at the head of the bed and since the walls of the room were papered with images of the devil and since I wanted salvation from all evil, that was all I could think of.

—TOMÁS RIVERA, author
"And the Earth Did Not Devour Him,"
Barrios and Borderlands

If we want [the church] to have a significant presence in Los Angeles, we have to see La Placita as a symbol of hope. What La Placita has been historically and what it must continue to be is an exaggerated symbol of the love of God for the poor.

—FATHER LUIS OLIVARES, pastor
LA Weekly, September 6–12, 1991

CREATIVITY

Chicano writers must begin using language creatively, movingly, and truthfully. Much of what passes for Chicano literature is dead imagery and boring symbols and rhetoric. If our writers lose their fear of language[s] and ideas, then will our literature flourish and inspire.
—RICARDO SÁNCHEZ, author

We must create out of our ashes. Our own hero must be born out of this wasteland, like the phoenix bird of the desert he must rise again from the ashes of our withered bodies.
—RUDOLFO ANAYA, author
Tortuga

As a group, we have to create the type of images that work for us, that totally capture who we are, not just the conditions we find ourselves in.
—PABLO FIGUEROA, filmmaker
Portraits

One's happiness is greatest when the story flows like a
stream of clear water, even if the worst abominations are
being narrated. It is only during the reading of those passages that the fear of what has flowed from one's own pen
takes over.

—LUISA VALENZUELA, author, educator
"Writing with the Body," *The Writer on Her Work*

Jumping barriers has been the story of my life. Most
people think of the obvious social and racial barriers, but
I've also been jumping barriers with respect to my art
form. When you're not visible, no one is accountable to
you. With film, I've built images that stand huge on the
landscape.

—LUIS M. VALDEZ, director, screenwriter
Rising Voices: Profiles in Leadership

My greatest gift, given to me by forces which confound
genetics, environment, race, or ambition, is a singing
voice. My second greatest gift, without which I would be
an entirely different person with an entirely different story
to tell, is a desire to share that voice, and the bounties it
has heaped upon me, with others. From that combination
of gifts has developed an immeasurable wealth—a wealth
of adventures, of friendships, and of plain joys.

—JOAN BAEZ, musician, activist
And a Voice to Sing With

Living in a state of psychic unrest, in a Borderland, is
what makes poets write and artists create.

—GLORIA ANZALDÚA, author
Borderlands/La Frontera: The New Mestiza

CUBA

The biggest crime in Cuba is to think.
—FRANCISCO RODRIGUEZ CRUZ, editor
Newsweek, May 26, 1980

We Cubans are a funny people, nostalgic, arrogant, and talkative. For example, it doesn't seem possible, but my children feel nostalgic for Cuba, my daughter especially. It's as if you could inherit nostalgia. . . . And do we like to talk! It's the national pastime. You know that the one thing you can't find in the Caribbean is a Cuban mime!
—HUMBERTO CALZADA, artist
Barrios and Borderlands

My parents really kept the myth and tradition of Cuba alive. That and places like Little Havana in Miami, where it is just like stepping into old Cuba.
—GLORIA ESTEFAN, musician
Entertainment Weekly, July 30, 1993

They have enough machismo and rhetoric in Cuba to last a lifetime. The new leader in Cuba should be a woman. It needs mothering.

—ANDY GARCÍA, actor
Redbook, January 1993

We lost our homeland. That's why those of us born in Cuba take democracy a lot more seriously than most.

—ILEANA ROS-LEHTINEN, congresswoman
Rising Voices: Profiles in Leadership

Castro is the devil in disguise. There is no liberty in Cuba, no human rights. My parents didn't want to raise me under that kind of government.

—JON SECADA, musician
People, July 11, 1994

[Cuban coffee is] very powerful, very sweet, and a little dangerous—just like the people who drink it.

—GLORIA ESTEFAN, musician
Entertainment Weekly, July 30, 1993

CULTURE

My culture is not without rhythm. It's a well-deserved stereotype in a way.

—ANDY GARCÍA, actor
Cosmopolitan, January 1990

The magazine [*Hispanic*] is a family business, so what keeps driving me is that it is my family's money at stake here. At the same time, the magazine is reflective of the growth in the Hispanic community. My hopes are that we will continue to grow and prosper.

—ALFREDO J. ESTRADA, editor, publisher
Rising Voices: Profiles in Leadership

But it is not really difference the oppressor fears so much as similarity.

—CHERRÍE MORAGA, author
"La Güera," *This Bridge Called My Back*

THE FIRE IN OUR SOULS

Now that I understand Latino behavior, it is clear that they don't fit the standard models of culture. Latinos push back with something against the low income and low level of education. And they push back so strongly and so persistently, that we have to look at the behavior and try to understand it.

—DAVID HAYES-BAUTISTA, editor
Rising Voices: Profiles in Leadership

As a card-carrying Chicano artist, I should know more about this holiday, but my family never really celebrated Los Muertos after coming here. It was Halloween all the way.

—LALO LOPEZ, journalist
"Mexiled," *LA Weekly*, October 27–November 2, 1995

Many Anglos have told me personally that they admire our way of life. I am sure others have confessed such. What is it that they admire—our poverty, our misery? No. They admire the way we cope with life and enjoy it. They admire our capacity to suffer and to enjoy. In a way they admire our freedom to be not so concerned with the damn future and with all these material possessions and trinkets which abound. The sense of loyalty to our *familias* and to friends. Even the rascal qualities we seem to have are at times admired, because we can be dishonest with flair rather than in the dark.

—ABELARDO DELGADO, educator

Culture

[My birth family] not only embraced me, but recognized my poetic spirit and told me all the stories that I already knew. But receiving them orally is different from finding them through dreams and the inner imagination.
—CLARISSA PINKOLA ESTES, author
San Francisco Chronicle, August 2, 1992

Whether we're Cuban-American, Mexican-American, Puerto Rican or Dominican, food is a central part of the Hispanic culture. While our food varies from fried plantains to tamales, what doesn't change is its role in our lives. You feed people you care for, and so if you're well cared for, *bien cuidada,* you have been fed well.
—CHRISTY HAUBEGGER, journalist
Essence, December 1994

[Commenting on those who criticized Detroit public radio station WDET-FM's cancellation of *El Grito de mi Raza*, a bilingual Hispanic cultural program:]
They echo those who say the melting pot model of American culture never worked. Many academics look at cultural diversity as a mosaic or tapestry where each part maintains its identity but is an integral part of the whole. Still many struggle to define how the tapestry fits together. Is it important to know that salsa is Latin-derived music? Or should we just enjoy it in our own context?
—LARRY GABRIEL, actor
Detroit Free Press, February 27, 1994

New generations discover that certain aspects of their national and cultural identity are so much a part of their inner selves that they are not free to give them up. The new mestizaje occurs when they take unto themselves the new culture while combining it with their own inner selves. If they return to their ancestral home, they quickly discover that they are now foreigners in their own land, for they have taken on the cultural personality of the new country. At first, this bicultural personality is difficult to live with, but in time it provides the basis for a new synthesis.

> —FATHER VIRGIL P. ELIZONDO, pastor
> "The Future Is Mestizo: Life Where Cultures Meet,"
> *Barrios and Borderlands*

We should acknowledge differences, we should greet differences, until difference makes no difference anymore.

> —DR. ADELA A. ALLEN, educator

Our history was so fragmented by colonialism that I have felt a mythology was needed, a putting together of everything in a modern sense. If you have a mythology, then you have a place; if you don't have a mythology, you ain't got nothing.

> —JIMMY SANTIAGO BACA, author
> *It's About Vision*

When a Cuban marries a Mexican, or a Puerto Rican marries a Venezuelan, that is considered to be inter-marriage. What will the familial pattern be between

Cubans and Mexicans at dinner? Will they eat *arroz con pollo* or *enchilada*? Instead of the answer being "both," I'd say "neither." The assumption that it is just another homogeneous marriage will just not be there.

—RODOLFO DE LA GARZA, professor
Hispanic, March 1994

My upbringing taught me that cultures are not isolated, and perish when deprived of contact with what is different and challenging. Reading, writing, teaching, learning, are all activities aimed at introducing civilizations to each other. No culture . . . retains its identity in isolation; identity is attained in contact, in contrast, in breakthrough.

—CARLOS FUENTES, author
"How I Started to Write"

Cultural variation among Chicanos is of fundamental importance. The Spanish-speaking population, who until the nineteenth century inhabited what is now the southwestern United States, shared a great many similarities with other colonial groups throughout Spanish America. The role of this group in establishing the foundations of Chicano culture, however, has yet to be properly acknowledged.

—GUILLERMO E. HERNÁNDEZ, professor
Chicano Satire

It is thus plausible, for example, for a family to include members with contrasting cultural features: that is, a woman imbued with a colonial cultural perspective married to a Mexican immigrant whose children identify themselves, their experiences, or aspirations as either Mexican, Mexican-American, Chicano, or Hispanic. Indeed, all these cultural or historical currents discussed ought not to be considered rigidly nor in isolation from each other.

—GUILLERMO E. HERNÁNDEZ, professor
Chicano Satire

There are so many features of the Chicano experience that are 100 percent eternal, that many people in the world can identify with. The strengths, our hopes, our family structure, our capacity to love, all the results of the closure of our society and what it has made of us. This vital and human experience could actually find readers, aside from the Americans, readers in Italy, Spain . . . because it is a universal one.

—ESTELA PORTILLO TRAMBLEY, author

Folk heroes arise of a need to articulate feelings unsung by conventionality.

—RUBEN SALAZAR, journalist
Los Angeles Times, July 17, 1970

Culture

In order to understand history and be able to exorcize the past, we need to relive in flesh and spirit this history. We need to reenact all the misunderstandings, confrontations and contradictions, all the suffering and havoc brought about by the so-called discovery of this continent by Europeans.

> —Francisco X. Alarcón, author
> "Reclaiming Ourselves, Reclaiming America," *Before Columbus Review, a Quarterly of Multicultural Literature*, Fall/Winter 1992

The United States had made me believe that we live only for the future; Mexico, Cardenas, the events of 1938, made me understand that only in an act of the present can we make present the past as well as the future: to be a Mexican was to identify a hunger for being, a desire for dignity rooted in many forgotten centuries and in many centuries yet to come, but rooted here, now, in the instant, in the vigilant time of Mexico I later learned to understand in the stone serpents of Teotihuacan and in the polychrome angels of Oaxaca.

> —Carlos Fuentes, author
> "How I Started to Write"

I had a great childhood in Miami Beach, but ultimately it's like having a stepmother. If you are uprooted from the womb of your real mother at the age of five, you can love your stepmother, but your mother is missing. You can't touch her, only love her from afar.

> —Andy García, actor
> *Redbook*, January 1993

By minimizing cultural differences, and portraying a false picture of unity, the dominant culture still tries to exert control and impose its values. It makes us an a-racial, a-cultural, a-theological church—and that's simply not true.

—BEN ALICÉA, associate director
Christianity Today, February 6, 1995

Now people have more of a chance and opportunity to go out and explore one's particular interests. Pursuing one's own interest has provided a greater trend toward acculturation. A lot of those family values [traditionally found among Hispanics] get somewhat diluted due to outside influence [brought] into the home.

—DR. CARLOS V. GRIJALVA, JR.,
psychologist
Hispanic, March 1994

[T]he cultural dilemma of the American of Mexican, Cuban or Puerto Rican descent is suddenly universalized: to integrate or not? to maintain a personality and add to the diversity of North American society, or to fade away into anonymity in the name of the after-all nonexistent "melting pot"? Well, perhaps the question is really, once more, to be or not to be? to be with others or to be alone? Isolation means death. Encounter means birth, even rebirth.

—CARLOS FUENTES, author
The Nation, March 30, 1992

Culture

People who are twice born as adoptees, especially if they are adopted into another culture, have the special ability to bridge those groups.
                    —CLARISSA PINKOLA ESTES, author
                    San Francisco Chronicle, August 2, 1992

DAY OF THE DEAD

Día de los Muertos has its roots in the Mexican (Aztec) culture where, through cleansing ceremonies and food offerings, the dead were honored and the living reminded how brief life really is. It was extra brief if you were next in line for the human sacrifice.

So, how do you celebrate [*Day of the Dead*]? 1. Build an altar to your favorite dead relative, friend or superstar. (I've seen the ultimate: a San Antonio, Texas, office with a Selena altar, complete with the slain singer's actual lip prints planted on a publicity photo!) 2. To the cemetery take *ofrendas*: some tamales for Grandma and perhaps a *cerveza* for your own spiritual nutrition. 3. Remember.

The standard *Día de los Muertos* or Day of the Dead altar has pictures of the deceased, items which remind you of the *muertito*, and *ofrendas*, plates of food, sweet bread and candles. You can set it up practically anywhere.

Day of the Dead

Día de Los Muertos exists not only to remind us that life is brief and illusory, but that it is to be cherished. It also reminds us that those loved ones who have gone before us can be as close as a plate of hot food, a can of cold beer or the flash of a bright memory.

—LALO LOPEZ, journalist
"Mexiled," *LA Weekly*, October 27–November 2, 1995

DISCRIMINATION

Discrimination may not be as overt as it used to be. There are no longer certain buses we can't get on, bars we can't go in, housing we can't rent. There are no longer signs that say "Keep out," but there might as well be.

—GLORIA MOLINA, county supervisor
Rising Voices: Profiles in Leadership

The minute I told him who I was and showed him the letter he himself had signed offering me steady work as a translator, he assumed a cold and impersonal attitude. He made it short and to the point. "Yes, I wrote that letter. I invited you to come to translate for us here at the office." And pointing to the other side of the room he added, "That was to be your desk and typewriter. But I thought you were white."

—JESÚS COLÓN, author, journalist
A Puerto Rican in New York

Discrimination

[A]s a whole it has gotten no better for the Hispanic in Hollywood. Things are far from ideal, but as a group we can no longer be dismissed or ignored by the Hollywood film community or the entertainment industry.

—EDWARD JAMES OLMOS, actor
Hispanic Hollywood

I remember when as children we attended movies in the nearby town of San Fernando where of the two movie theatres, Mexicans were welcome in one, the Towne Theatre. The other, El Rennie Theatre, catered to Anglos and was off limits to *chicanada* of Pacoima and Sanfer. It was not until World War II and soon after that Mexican-Americans (as we were then known) became socially acceptable at local movies and restaurants. Many barrio men were wounded, killed and decorated while fighting for their country, the good ole USA. It was not considered patriotic to turn away non-whites in uniform so we were let inside.

—MERRIHELEN PONCE ADAME, poet, author
"Chochis and the Movies at Sanfer,"
The Southern California Anthology 1984

Prejudice is a state of mind that can be cured with success.

—FRANSISCO AVELAR, educator

In [the United States], having a French or German accent is to be considered cultured, educated. But if you have a Spanish accent you are ignored, even if you are a Ph.D.

—attributed to HUGO PIÑEDA, author

One can only imagine the public outcry if law enforcement officials had the authority to board public transportation and single out and interrogate Jews or African Americans. Yet, this anti-right is a reality for Latinos, near the border and, increasingly, even for those not living near the border.

—ROBERTO RODRIGUEZ, filmmaker,
and PATRISIA GONZALES, author *Latino Spectrum*

From the employment office I would call door to door at the piers, factories and storage houses in the streets under the Brooklyn and Manhattan Bridges. "Sorry, nothing today." It seemed to me that that "today" was a continuation and combination of all the yesterdays, todays and tomorrows.

From the factories I would go to the restaurants looking for a job as a porter or dishwasher. At least I would eat and be warm in a kitchen.

"Sorry" . . . "Sorry" . . .

—JESÚS COLÓN, author, journalist
A Puerto Rican in New York

The most important reason why Hispanics remain a people apart is that they are different from others in the U.S. Church. Though other ethnic groups did encounter short-term discrimination, Hispanics were rejected outright. They underwent a process that left them "colonized," "conquered," "strangers in their own land." The defeatism which is the chief effect of that sad history leaves many unable to associate on an equal basis with members of the majority culture. Though much healing has taken place in recent years, it will be a long time before the process is complete.

—MOISÉS SANDOVAL, journalist
Barrios and Borderlands

So there I was [in junior high school in Redlands, California], with a Mexican name, skin and hair: the Anglos couldn't accept me because of all three, and the Mexicans couldn't accept me because I didn't speak Spanish.

—JOAN BAEZ, musician, activist
And a Voice to Sing With

Possession of crack cocaine is treated much more harshly than possession of powdered cocaine. Coincidentally, crack is generally preferred by black and brown inner-city youth, whereas powdered cocaine is preferred by suburban whites and the better off.

—ROBERTO RODRIGUEZ, filmmaker,
and PATRISIA GONZALES, author *Latino Spectrum*

Yesterday, I was in Austin waiting for my plane, and there was a young man and a young woman there. Everyone's waiting for the plane, and she is eating breakfast. What is she eating for breakfast? Flour tortillas with whatever is mixed up in it—just what Tony is being made fun of for eating in *Bless Me, Ultima*. And I thought, "Isn't that nice?" Now that the majority of the population has legitimized eating tacos for breakfast, it's perfectly OK even to eat them in airports. But the sad part of the scene in *Bless Me, Ultima* is that the kids who are making fun of Tony are also Mexicans. They're little city boys from that little town and they're poking fun at this rural Mexican who's eating tacos.

—ROLANDO HINOJOSA-SMITH, author
*Interviews with Writers of the
Post-Colonial World, 1992*

When I was mayor, we had to spend a lot of time doing surveys indicating that there was discrimination against minority contractors. And I now realize that we didn't have a lot of support from the federal government, we didn't have a lot of direction, we didn't have a lot of encouragement. And now that I'm here, I want to make sure that we provide that support and encouragement to people around the country.

—FEDERICO PEÑA, Secretary of Transportation
Hispanic, June 1993

These bullets bury deeper than logic / Racism is not intellectual. / I can not reason these scars away . . . Everyday I am deluged with reminders / that this is not / my land / and this is my land. I do not believe in the war between the races / but in this country / there is war.

—LORNA DEE CERVANTES, editor, poet
"Poem for the Young White Man Who Asked Me
How I, an Intelligent, Well-Read Person Could Believe
in the War Between Races," *In Other Words,
Literature by Latinas of the United States*

Discrimination

But let me tell you about prejudice. It starts in the home, and that's in all cultures, all races, all creeds. The only thing we can do, as educated people, is understand that we do have these feelings and say to ourselves, "Hey, that's racist, I don't have to think that way."
—EDWARD JAMES OLMOS, actor
Los Angeles Magazine, April 1993

I would visit the government employment office on Jay Street. The conversations among the Puerto Ricans on the large wooden benches in the employment office were always on the same subject. How to find a decent place to live. How they would not rent to Negroes or Puerto Ricans. How Negroes and Puerto Ricans were given the pink slips first at work.
—JESÚS COLÓN, author, journalist
A Puerto Rican in New York

The proliferation of anti-rights sentiment is due to a movement based on prejudice that seeks to curb the rights and liberties of groups and individuals it considers less than human—generally people of color.
—ROBERTO RODRIGUEZ, filmmaker,
and PATRISIA GONZALES, author *Latino Spectrum*

EDUCATION

Yes, it's emotionally and psychologically difficult to get involved in anything when you don't know where your next meal is coming from. Nonetheless, education is the solution to cyclical poverty and Latinas in particular need to concentrate on the solution, not the problem!

—BETTINA R. FLORES, author
Chiquita's Cocoon

Growing up where I did [Las Vegas, New Mexico] and seeing the desperate need for education among people who looked like me made me believe that we could break the poverty hold on Chicanos if we educated ourselves. I started reaching out to help and it became a way of life.

—MARI-LUCI JARAMILLO, educator, diplomat
Notable Hispanic American Women

Education

You don't need anything else more than the desire to learn, which I call *ganas*.

—JAIME ESCALANTE, educator

Information is power. We are changing from an industrial to an information-driven society and we cannot be left behind. We need to prepare our people to become information producers.

—JOSE MONTES DE OCA, businessman
Hispanic, March 1995

"Oh, please tell me what my son will be," my mother glanced anxiously from me to Ultima.
"He will be a man of learning," Ultima said sadly.
"¡Madre de Dios!" my mother cried and crossed herself.

—RUDOLFO ANAYA, author
Bless Me, Ultima

It is clear that lack of education is the main barrier confronting Hispanics in their effort to attain full entry into the American mainstream.

—ILEANA ROS-LEHTINEN, congresswoman
Rising Voices: Profiles in Leadership

How many times have we read boastful statements from high educational leaders in our big newspapers that while other countries ignore the history and culture of the United States, our educational system does instruct our children in the history and traditions of other cultures.

As far as instruction in the most elementary knowledge of Latin America is concerned, we are forced to state that what our children receive is a hodgepodge of romantic generalities and chauvinistic declarations spread further and wider by Hollywood movies.

—JESÚS COLÓN, author, journalist
A Puerto Rican in New York

You've never heard of four Ph.D.'s doing a drive-by or of four engineers holding up a liquor store.

—JAIME OAXACA, businessman

I used to think that if you educate people, they will be able to make it. I found out that it isn't so. Some highly educated people cannot get into the system for a variety of reasons. Today I counsel students to learn about the importance of economics and the political aspects of our democracy regardless of their field of expertise. "Know the system and make it work for you," I tell them. You have to understand how the business world operates and what it means when our government talks about protecting American interests in a foreign country. You have to see yourself in relation to current events in order to participate.

—MARI-LUCI JARAMILLO, educator, diplomat
Notable Hispanic American Women

Struggle to learn, learn to struggle.

—FRANK BONILLA, professor
Portraits

Now my children go to American high schools. / They speak English. At night they sit around / the kitchen table, laugh with one another. / I stand by the stove and feel dumb, alone. / I bought a book to learn English.

—PAT MORA, author
"Elena," *Barrios and Borderlands*

That's the point. It goes like this: Teaching is touching life.

—JAIME ESCALANTE, educator
Technos, Spring 1993

FAMILY

In the modern world, the Hispanic family has experienced all the mainstream disruption that America has and perhaps more, due to their socioeconomic position.

—RODOLFO DE LA GARZA, professor
Hispanic, March 1994

When my little boy, Dimitri, died, everybody was crying. Me? I got up, and I danced. They said, "Zorba is mad." But it was the dancing—only the dancing—that stopped the pain. You see, he was my first. He was only three. When I'm happy, it's the same thing.

—ANTHONY QUINN, actor
in *Zorba the Greek*

It's been my dream for many years to make a film about a Latino family. We aren't just individuals; we are each a product of our families.

Family

Familia is the very center of Latino culture. I don't feel the media has really seen that. It is the strongest thing about us and the most universal.
—GREGORY NAVA, filmmaker
Los Angeles Magazine, May 1995

I am the product of a heritage that teaches strong family devotion, a commitment to earning a livelihood by hard work, patience, determination and perseverance.
—KATHERINE DAVALOS ORTEGA, former
Treasurer of the United States
*Roots of Greatness: The 1995 Mexican-American
Historical Calendar*

What the statistics don't tell us is the closeness of the relationship. Hispanic families are very cohesive, spending much time together.
—MERCEDES ALVAREZ, businesswoman
Hispanic, March 1994

Warning! This Latin family is not representative of all Latin families—not even some Latin families. It's a unique and individual case. If your family is like this one, please seek professional help.
—JOHN LEGUIZAMO, actor
Spic-O-Rama . . . A Dysfunctional Comedy

There was a dream I used to have about you and I. It was always the same. I'd be told that you were dead, and I would run crying into the street. Someone would stop and ask, "Why are you crying?" and I would say, "Because my father is dead, and he never said he loved me."

—MARTIN SHEEN, actor
in *The Subject Was Roses*

HOLLYWOOD

I love the United States of America, and I love living here. But as an actor and as an individual, I find myself in a dual position. Like others from Latin America, I am part of an alien nation within a larger nation. . . . The fruits of our labor are prized and needed, but we are kept apart, due to our language and culture. They like our food and admire our colorful art, but do not accept us as peers. Even in Hollywood, and not even after decades of positive change in other arenas.

—RAMÓN NOVARRO, actor
Hispanic Hollywood

There were three perpetrations that upset me. *House of the Spirits*—no Latins, *Death and the Maiden*—no Latins, and *The Perez Family*—no Latins. It's ridiculous, man, with all the Latins we have. It's shameful. But I also want to put across to Latin people that we have got to be more aggressive, more vocal. We can't let people walk all over us any more, and we let it happen. It's our fault this is happening to us.

—JOHN LEGUIZAMO, actor
Hispanic, May 1995

We lack role models because we don't have a medium that we can look to for *lo nuestro*. Do you know any Hispanics who are on sitcoms, in the movies, on soaps? Maybe a tiny handful. That's not enough. My question is, why are talented Hispanics being held down exclusively to the Hispanic market? I just don't get it.

—DAISY FUENTES, educator
Hispanic, August 1993

I didn't want to be anchor-woman. Puhleasse. I had a chip on my shoulder. . . . I thought, "Oh, these people just want a token Hispanic."

—NELY GALÁN, producer

We need to send a message to ABC-TV and the other three networks that unless they begin to include us in their prime-time shows with positive portrayals, we will not watch their programs or patronize those who sponsor them.

—ALEX NOGALES, National Hispanic Media Coalition
Hispanic Business, October 1995

Television tells children where they are in society. If you're not on TV, you're not important. And right now we're still very unimportant.

—ESTHER RENTERÍA, businesswoman
Latino Spectrum

An actor must be regarded as an actor and he must be given the opportunity to prove that he can play any role, whether it's part of his background or not. Unfortunately, many of the people in casting and producing and directing see actors only as types. So the actor must constantly fight the limitations others want to put on him.

—RAÚL JULIA, actor
Hispanics in Hollywood

At first, for a long time, screen Hispanics were bandits or lovers. Then we were ignored. Today we are under-represented, and often misrepresented, but due to our increasing numbers, we are ignored less and less.

—RICARDO MONTALBÁN, actor
Hispanic Hollywood

It wasn't easy. I was terrified at first. I knew I had to get out of town because there was too much temptation here. I could have taken any of those spitfire roles and made a bundle. Luckily, I was so demeaned—it's really demeaning after you've won the Oscar to be offered the same role over and over again. They only wanted me to drag out my accent-and-dance show over and over again. And boy, I was offered them all—gypsy fortune-tellers, Mexican spitfires, Spanish spitfires, Puerto Ricans—all those "Yonkee peeg, you steal me people's money" parts. The only thing I could do was turn my back on it.

—RITA MORENO, actress
Hispanic Hollywood

In an ideal situation, all artists should be able to play any role. But we don't live in an ideal world. Before, our stories weren't told. Now, great [Latino] stories are being told and we can't play ourselves.

—ESTHER RENTERÍA, businesswoman
Latino Spectrum

We are not demanding jobs as actors and technicians in the entertainment industry merely because we are of Spanish origin, but we are insisting that we not be excluded from consideration because our surnames happen to be Gonzalez, Lopez, or even Montalbán.

—RICARDO MONTALBÁN, actor
Famous Mexican-Americans

When the few good Latin parts go to non-Hispanic actors, Hollywood is saying, "You people are interesting enough to make films about, but you're not good enough to play yourselves."

—JOHN LEGUIZAMO, actor
Premier, August 1992

I am very hurt that I am not considered an American actor, extremely hurt by it. But I'm afraid the die has been cast, and I will have to play these ethnic roles—but I must say, I'm very happy, because I get to play Hungarians, I get to play Turkish, I get to play Chinese, I get to play Russians—I get to play a much wider scope of humanity than just, quote, American.

—ANTHONY QUINN, actor
Hispanics in Hollywood

During the first few decades of talkies, if you spoke Spanish, more if your parents did, you were treated as local color and stuck behind a boulder or inside a barroom.

—ANTONIO MORENO, actor
In View

What would be nice is if, in the future, there can be Hispanics who can be Hispanic and just play people, like Caucasians are able to do. Hopefully, such delineations will go away. They're of absolutely no relevance. The only time in my life when I've confronted the issue about being Hispanic is when it comes to casting, not in my normal life, only in what television and the media seem to perceive Hispanics as being. The more that we can hold that out there as happening, without putting too much emphasis on it, the better for all of us.

—ROXANNE BIGGS-DAWSON, actress
Hispanic, April 1995

The lack of Latinos [on television and other media] reinforces their image as an invisible population. Television tells us what we are, what we're worth, where we're going. If we're invisible, what does that say about how important we are?

—ALEX NOGALES, National Hispanic Media Coalition
Hispanic Business, October 1995

Now and then a few good pictures get made, thanks to a persistent and well-connected producer or director. But oddly enough, it's the good pictures Hollywood is most afraid of.

—FERNANDO LAMAS, actor
Hispanic Hollywood

I'm Puerto Rican and that in itself seems to mean spitfire to so many people in Hollywood. It's tough enough getting roles being a woman, but being both female and Puerto Rican makes it all that much harder. I think barriers, the stereotypes, actually are finally falling apart. I want to show that I can play several kinds of roles, not just Latinas, though I look forward to good Latina parts.

—RITA MORENO, actress
San Francisco Chronicle, September 14, 1976

The industry is run on economics. It knows only one color: green. There's prejudice, sure. But economics makes it go away.

—EDWARD JAMES OLMOS, actor
Time, July 11, 1988

To me, these serials were a gold mine. I was the first to wish the hero eternal life—the longer the serials, the more money I could earn [translating the screen subtitles for silent films].

—Jesús Colón, author, journalist
A Puerto Rican in New York

[On watching a satiric World War II propaganda film:]
I remember thinking it was wrong to make fun of other ethnic groups. We were not exactly blonde and blue-eyed. We were brown. Light and dark brown, but nonetheless, brown. Morenos, triguenos, prietos. Not white enough to be accepted in the predominantly white Rennie Theatre, but able to laugh at others who like our ancestors had fought a war against this country, men who had been mocked and called "dirty Mexicans" not "dirty Japs."

—Merrihelen Ponce Adame, poet, author
"Chochis and the Movies at Sanfer,"
The Southern California Anthology 1984

This film about our people [*Stand and Deliver*] will touch the nation. It shows we can achieve anything we want. Being able to make a film like this is the finest moment of my life.

—Edward James Olmos, actor
Los Angeles Times, March 27, 1988

The people who control the movie business, generally—there are exceptions, I hope—see it as a product. It's more like salespeople packaging a product. They're not very concerned with what the movie contributes to people. They're not very much concerned with the human values that can be posed or explored in a film. They are shoe sellers making films.

—RAÚL JULIA, actor
Washington Post, 1985

There were more Hispanic faces in the movies and on TV when I was growing up than there are now. According to a recent study, the rate of Hispanics [working in Hollywood] has gone down since the fifties and sixties, which is *amazing*. When I was a kid I could see Pepino on *The Real McCoys*, or actors like Anthony Quinn, Gilbert Roland, and Dolores Del Rio in their films. There was a lot of visibility for Hispanics then. There were enough role models, though I wasn't thinking about it at the time, for me to think, "Hey, if they can do it, maybe I can, too."

—ROBERT BELTRÁN, actor
Hispanic, April 1995

[Commenting on having served Jon Voight at the Annual Golden Globe Awards:]
You're always just a salad plate away.

—ANDY GARCÍA, actor
Redbook, January 1993

[On silent movie weekly serials:]

The idea was to excite enough curiosity for you to return next week to see what surely appeared, from all logical deduction, like certain death for the hero or heroine. But—what do you know! She or he was miraculously saved from a horrible ending by one of the thousand props that the director always had ready to extract from his shirt sleeve and the serial went on and on for months.

—JESÚS COLÓN, author, journalist
A Puerto Rican in New York

HUMAN RIGHTS

You cannot be witness to the human suffering and not be convinced of the existence of social sin. We are all responsible unless we take a stand and speak out against it.
—FATHER LUIS OLIVARES, pastor

My commitment is to have my nation free . . . not as a political fanatic but as a human rights visionary. As an artist I can't avoid presenting some of my work as a narrator of things that are happening today in Puerto Rico.
—DENNIS MARIO RIVERA, artist
Hispanic, January/February 1995

The first law is the one of human dignity.
—FATHER LUIS OLIVARES, pastor
sermon advocating the Sanctuary movement, 1985

Internationally, I find these so-called ethnic cleansings that have been carried out in Eastern Europe, these so-called "wars of conscience" extremely disturbing. This idea of ethnic groups claiming the right to live apart and by themselves spells trouble all over the world.
—RITA RICARDO-CAMPBELL, senior fellow
Hoover Institution Newsletter, Winter 1988–1989

Although we are not above the law, the struggle of undocumented people to assert their rights as human beings *is*.
—FATHER LUIS OLIVARES, pastor
Los Angeles Times, December 1986

IDENTITY

In this autobiographical account [*Hunger of Memory*], [Richard] Rodriguez asserts his Americanism by pointing out every possible social and cultural element that no longer identifies him as a Mexican. Drawing from his individual experience, Rodriguez portrays himself as a cultural martyr whose assimilation has led to alienation from his parents, his studies, and his cultural roots. . . . Rodriguez's basic tenet is that total Chicano assimilation into Anglo-American life represents the only viable alternative for children of Mexican immigrants.

—GUILLERMO E. HERNÁNDEZ, professor
Chicano Satire

The Gringo, locked into the fiction of white superiority, seized complete political power, stripping Indians and Mexicans of their land while their feet were still rooted in it. *Con el destierro y el exilio fuimos desuñados, destroncados, destripados*—we were jerked out by the roots, truncated, disemboweled, dispossessed, and separated from our identity and history.

—GLORIA ANZALDÚA, author
Borderlands/La Frontera: The New Mestiza

I live smack in the fissure between two worlds, in the infected wound: half a block from the end of Western Civilization and four miles from the start of the Mexican-American border, the northernmost point of Latin America. In my fractured reality, but a reality nonetheless, there cohabit two historical languages, cosmologies, artistic traditions, and political systems which are drastically counterposed.

—GUILLERMO GÓMEZ-PEÑA, performance artist
"Documented/Undocumented," *LA Weekly*

I didn't realize until I left New York and went to college that, number one, I might be Caucasian but I wasn't white, and number two, New York may be the world in microcosm but it gives you no perspective whatsoever on the rest of the country.

—CARLOS GAIVAR, journalist

I am visible—see this Indian face—yet I am invisible. I both blind them with my beak nose and am their blind spot. But I exist, we exist. They'd like to think I have melted in the pot. But I haven't, we haven't.

—GLORIA ANZALDÚA, author
"La Conciencia de la Mestiza/Towards a New Consciousness," *In Other Words, Literature by Latinas of the United States*

As they drove home through the dark streets, Margo tasted humiliation, bitter as gall, rising again in her throat, in a surge of self-loathing. The next moment, though, she thought, "I can't go on like this for the rest of my life. I am who I am. If others don't like me, it's their problem. I belong in this country as much as they do, down here even more than they because we were here first."

—Beatriz de la Garza, author
"Margarita," *In Other Words, Literature by Latinas of the United States*

Basically, "gringo" is an attitude. Blacks have called it racism or honky. In South America or the Far East, it's called "yankee imperialism." It's the whole paternalistic, ethnocentric, xenophobic attitude. It's typical among people who come from sections of Europe of Anglo-Saxon origin. You call them bigots, racists, animals. We Chicanos use the word "gringos."

—Jose Angel Gutiérrez, judge
Famous Mexican-Americans

The great pain of *mestizo* culture—Mexicans, Salvadorans, Chicanos, etc.—is the constant feeling of living in exile, that there is no one "home" possible for us. Its redemption is the realization that the entire world is our home.

—Rubén Martínez
LA Weekly, June 1993

I feel very strongly that Mexican-Americans—and I hate the use of the hyphen but I can't do anything about it—have a responsibility to participate in the mainstream of American life, but they still do not have to forsake the heritage of their culture or their language. . . . We cannot have it both ways. We cannot say, "I have the right to segregate and to set myself apart, but you must not discriminate if I do."

—HENRY B. GONZALEZ, congressman
Famous Mexican-Americans

I can attest to the fact that [in the late 1940s and early 1950s] having a new car was almost like adopting a new family member. There was pride that went into having a car. It was a status symbol for a lot of Chicanos of that era. . . . As Chicanos we refuse to assimilate. There's something that breaks us apart from the mainstream. That same idea translated to the cars.

—ALBERTO LOPEZ, publisher
Hispanic, July 1994

The diverse meanings of the word Hispanic reflect a heterogeneity that the word obscures. In New Mexico, Hispanic refers only to the descendants of the Spaniards who settled there in the 16th century. In the East, Hispanic is the generic term for people with Spanish surnames, although some consider Hispanic to be an elitist term. Therefore, many with Spanish surnames prefer Latino to Hispanic as the generic term of identification.

—JOANNE POTTLITZER, author
Hispanic Theater in the United States and Puerto Rico

I don't know if the barrio can any more be the focus of our community. The Chicano is entering the mainstream, the middle class. There is no doubt about that. There are people who will argue it, but by and large, that's the drive. And it brings up one more cycle of our history. We are wrapped up as part of the human condition in cycles. The important thing, I think, is to look at this new cycle.

—RUDOLFO ANAYA, author
Interviews with Writers of the Post-Colonial World, 1992

I grew up in a New York neighborhood surrounded by seven or eight cultures—Puerto Rican, Jewish, Italian, Irish, you name it. All this soaked in like a sponge. For me, ethnic was wonderful. I'm known as "the man of a thousand races"!

—HECTOR ELIZONDO, actor
USA Today, 1986

There is a tremendous gap between the Hispanic market that watches Spanish language television and the untapped market that knows who Gabriel García Márquez is. You need one for survival; you need the other for our future. The gap must be bridged.

—NELY GALÁN, producer

There is no force which can divide Hispanics and Blacks. We share the same problems and, despite our cultural differences, we seek the same solutions. I am first, and above all, a Puertorriqueño.

—ROBERT GARCÍA, congressman
Portraits

I'm proud to be Afro-Cuban American. I wanted to make an album that says, "I am a black man."

—JON SECADA, musician
People, July 11, 1994

Identity

I write the myths in me, the myths I am, the myths I want to become. The word, the image and the feeling have a palatable energy, a kind of power. *Con imagenes domo mi miedo, cruzo los abismos que tengo por dentro. Con palabras me hago piedra, pajaro, puente de serpientes arrastrando a ras del suelo todo lo que soy, todo lo que algun dia sere.*

—GLORIA ANZALDÚA, author
Borderlands/La Frontera: The New Mestiza

What are the common denominators that unite the people? The real common denominator is nationalism. And when I say this some people run around in their intellectual bags and yell "reverse racism."

—RODOLFO "CORKY" GONZÁLES, activist
Famous Mexican-Americans

I was raised in what I consider to be not a melting pot, but a salad bowl. The onion stayed the onion, the tomato stayed the tomato, the lettuce stayed the lettuce, with maybe a little Russian or Italian dressing. And it tasted real good. No one lost their identity, and I thought that was what life was like.

—EDWARD JAMES OLMOS, actor
Los Angeles Times, May 10, 1992

Blacks and whites, Jews and gentiles. Hindus, Krauts, Spics and orientiles. This barrio used to be a dandy neighborhood. But since they moved in with their Voo-doo Hoo-doo. Since they moved in, there went the neighborhood!

—DOLORES PRIDA, author
Barrios and Borderlands

There is worse than pain.
There is forgetting
Those are my eyes in the mirror.
There is forgetting my own true name.
          —PAT MORA, author
          "Tigua Elder," *In Other Words, Literature
          by Latinas of the United States*

If you are a Chicano writer you are bound to be in a constant struggle with yourself to sort out what it is that you say that has actually been influenced by the way the Raza you represent thinks. The other side of that coin is that we are constantly influenced . . . by the way Anglos think. That struggle is bound to be reflected in what we write. . . . The humiliation of having to be at the mercy of a crumb-throwing society and even the acceptance of the role of adopting *nueva lengua* [a new language] and the idea of being on your own soil as a foreigner . . . all of these things have to be a set of themes with universal relationship, but with a very peculiar Chicano flavor. We drown in two cultures and when we come up for air for a third time we do not know whether to yell for help or *auxilio*.
          —ABELARDO DELGADO, educator

We will consider our jobs done when every one of our people recognizes his sense of personal dignity and pride in his history, his culture and his race.
          —LUÍS M. VALDEZ, director, screenwriter
          "El Teatro Campesino," *Roots of Greatness: The 1995
          Mexican-American Historical Calendar*

"Hispanic" is English for a person of Latino origin who wants to be accepted by the white status quo. Latino is the word we have always used for ourselves.

    —SANDRA CISNEROS, author
        quoted by Mary B. W. Tabor in volume 1 of *Hispanic Literature Criticism*

When I was in college, I made a trip to Mexico. . . . For the first time, I was in a place where people like me were the beautiful ones. And I began to accept, and even like, this body that I have.

    —CHRISTY HAUBEGGER, journalist
    Essence, December 1994

A Chicano is a Mexican American with a non-Anglo self-image.

    —RUBÉN SALAZAR, journalist
    Roots of Greatness

Our father, the Spaniard, left us. We decided to stay with our mother, the Indian, here in New Mexico. . . . We were born as the consequences of a conflict of races and cultures, when the Spanish discovered, explored, and Christianized this continent. Out of that conflict came a New Breed, a new people. Sometimes we are known as La Raza, which is the Race, the People. But the name we are known by does not matter. We are a New Breed.

    —REIS LÓPEZ TIJERINA, activist
    "Voices of La Causa"

Finally, through struggle and suffering the new identity will begin to emerge and the self will be able to shout out with joy: "I am." This new identity does not eliminate either the original culture of the parents or the culture of the new country. On the contrary, it enriches both by opening up each to the possibilities of the other.

> —FATHER VIRGIL P. ELIZONDO, pastor
> "The Future Is Mestizo: Life Where Cultures Meet,"
> *Barrios and Borderlands*

The words Chicano and Mexican American also evoke different connotations. The term Chicano has been in common usage in California and the Southwest for generations; some believe it derives from the word *Mexicano*. It frequently connotes political activism among Mexican Americans.

> —JOANNE POTTLITZER, author
> *Hispanic Theater in the United States and Puerto Rico*

I am what I am and you can't take it away with all the words and sneers at your command I am what I am I am Puerto Rican I am U.S. American . . . I am what I am and I'm naturalized Jewish American wasp is foreign and new but Jewish-American is old shoe familiar Shmata familiar and it's me dears it's me bagels and all I am what I am Take it or leave me alone.

> —ROSARIO MORALES, author
> "I Am What I Am," *Barrios and Borderlands*

Identity

Released from your cell
yet prisoner on your island
Write us books
to rediscover our identity
>—SANDRA MARIA ESTEVES, author, artist
>"For Lolita Lebron," *Puerto Rican Writers at Home in the USA*

I am new. History made me. My first language was spanglish. / I was born at the crossroads / and I am whole.
>—AURORA LEVINS MORALES, author
>"Child of the Americas," *Barrios and Borderlands*

Unlike her mother, who repeatedly claimed "some Spanish blood," Amalia did not welcome it when people she did housework for referred to her—carefully—as "Spanish." She was proud to be Mexican-American.
>—JOHN RECHY, author
>*The Miraculous Day of Amalia Gómez*

I really embraced the Mexican culture, not in a radical way. But I definitely didn't want to turn my back on it and be considered totally homogeneous with the American culture. It's been an interesting balance I've tried to keep all my life.
>—TISH HINOJOSA, musician
>*Hispanic*, January/February 1994

To separate from my culture (as from my family) I had to feel competent enough on the outside and secure enough inside to live life on my own. Yet in leaving home, I did not lose touch with my origins because *lo mexicano* is in my system. I am a turtle, wherever I go I carry "home" on my back.

> —GLORIA ANZALDÚA, author
> *Borderlands/La Frontera: The New Mestiza*

Tell me who you keep company with and I'll tell you who you are.

> —a mother's proverb
> *Roots of Greatness*

The fear that Latinas will deny their heritage if they leave home is a myth. If you want to be a Latina, Chicana, Mexican or Hispana, you can be one anywhere. Leaving home has very little to do with denying one's heritage and much to do with emotional blackmail.

> —BETTINA R. FLORES, author
> *Chiquita's Cocoon*

In the "Danger Zone" we live in, the South faces off with the North, man with woman, gay with straight, English with Spanish, the person of faith with the atheist, the artist-activist and the aesthete. We can accept or deny this truth: That the Mexican identity crisis is the same as the "culture wars" in the U.S., that the Indian in Mexico lives substantially the same reality as the immigrant in California, that the nativist in the U.S. is the twin of the one that

marginalizes the Indian in Mexico. We can no longer see the U.S. and Mexico as separated by an absurd line on a map, by a river filled with the blood of history. Today, we all live in the "Danger Zone."
>—RUBÉN MARTÍNEZ, author
>from the artistic manifesto "The Danger Zone We All Live In," part of the Danger Zone/Terreno Peligroso Binational Performance Art Festival, Mexico City–Los Angeles, February 1995

Today, eight years after my departure [from Mexico], when they ask me for my nationality or ethnic identity, I can't respond with one word, since my "identity" now possesses multiple repertories: I am Mexican but I am also Chicano and Latin American. At the border they call me *chilango* or *mexiquillo*; in Mexico City it's *pocho* or *norteño*; and in Europe it's *sudaca*. The Anglos call me "Hispanic" or "Latino," and the Germans have, on more than one occasion, confused me with Turks or Italians.
>—GUILLERMO GÓMEZ-PEÑA, performance artist
>"Documented/Undocumented," *English Broken Here*

Mine is the generation that arrived too late for Che Guevara, but too early for the fall of the Berlin Wall. Weaned on a blend of cultures, languages and ideologies, I've lived both in the north and the south, trying to be south in the south, north in the north, south in the north and north in the south. Now I stand at the center, watching history whirl around me as my own history fissures. . . . I can't decide if what I see is a beginning or an end.
>—RUBÉN MARTÍNEZ, author
>*The Other Side: Notes from the New Los Angeles, Mexico City and Beyond*

THE FIRE IN OUR SOULS

Is the Anglo really the enemy? Or is the enemy our fear of the unknown and our reluctance to conquer it? Yes, Anglos, or anyone else for that matter, can intimidate you, make you feel inferior and threaten you, but only when they are more knowledgeable than you and only when you let them.

—BETTINA R. FLORES, author
Chiquita's Cocoon

I have been obsessed, for the better part of my adult life, with questions of cultural identity and its relationship to the history of California. In my 31 years, I have played the role of an accentless, perfectly assimilated American kid. But I've also betrayed my parents' and grandparents' ideals of assimilation. I have returned to the Old Countries (my father's Mexico, my mother's El Salvador); I have on occasion proclaimed myself separate from Anglo-American culture; I've been known to warn Anglos that they just might be the ones who are going to get deported—back to Europe—when I hear them talking about deporting my Latin American brothers and sisters. . . .

I have also dreamed of a California in which a historical wound hundreds of years old might be healed: a reconciliation between north and south, the Catholic and the Protestant, the First and Third worlds. I've come to admit that rock 'n' roll is as important to my spiritual well-being as *la Virgen de Guadalupe*. I will always be the outsider in Latin America. I also oftentimes feel like an outcast in the United States. The only place I could be at home is in the new—the almost new—California.

—RUBÉN MARTÍNEZ, author
"The Dance of Nuevo L.A.," *Los Angeles Times Magazine*, January 30, 1994

Identity

When you are poor, painting your house, putting up a shrine to the Virgin of Guadalupe, or even tagging becomes the way that you can confirm your identity.

> —GUSTAVO LECLERC, architect, artist
> "Stylemakers," *L.A. Style*, 1994

The endangered are not species.
The endangered is beauty,
Unfrozen.

> —BERNICE ZAMORA, author
> *In Other Words, Literature by*
> *Latinas of the United States*

IMMIGRATION

The U.S.-Mexican border, some of those who cross it say, is not really a border but a scar. Will it heal? Will it bleed once more? When a Hispanic worker crosses this border, he sometimes asks, "Hasn't this always been our land? Am I not coming back to it? Is it not in some way ours?" He can taste it, hear its language, sing its songs and pray to its saints. Will his not always be a Hispanic land?
>   —CARLOS FUENTES, author
>   *The Nation*, March 30, 1992

stupid america, see that chicano / with a big knife / in his steady hand / he doesn't want to knife you / he wants to sit on a bench / and carve christfigures / but you won't let him.
>   —ABELARDO DELGADO, author
>   "stupid america," *Dictionary of Literary Biography*

Immigration

People think of the Latino population here as recently arrived. But the oldest neighborhoods in town are the Mexican neighborhoods—because it used to be Mexico.

—GREGORY NAVA, filmmaker
Los Angeles Magazine, May 1995

I looked at [a dead illegal alien] and I thought something woke up in me. I got enlightened. I made a vow. I decided I ain't hassling people who look like me. It ain't right. It's got to stop. I don't want to fight or arrest people who look like him. But I've got to follow orders. So . . . I'm going to pull everyone who looks like an alien. . . . They could be illegal British or illegal Norwegian aliens or illegal Canadian aliens taking hockey jobs from Americans.

—RICK NAJERA, comedian
The Pain of the Macho

When I first came to Miami [in 1960], you'd see signs like "No Children, No Pets, No Cubans." We were a major threat. We lived in a very small apartment behind the Orange Bowl, where all the Cubans lived. All the men (including my father, Jose Manuel Fajardo) were political prisoners in Cuba, and it was purely women and their kids. There was one car the whole community bought for $50, and the one lady that could drive would take everybody to the supermarket and the Laundromat.

—GLORIA ESTEFAN, musician
Entertainment Weekly, July 30, 1993

Children [born in the United States] of undocumented workers should not be held responsible for the actions of their parents. These proposals [to deny them citizenship] violate the most fundamental right anyone born in this country has.

—RAÚL YZAGUIRRE, public official
Hispanic Link Weekly Report, January 8, 1996

Public assistance/welfare, crime and a lack of education is the syndrome of failure in the immigrant community.

—FRANSISCO AVELAR, educator

[Commenting on a congressional proposal to deny citizenship to children born in the United States of undocumented workers:]
This is part of a misguided anti-immigrant policy going on in Congress. If this complaint involved immigrants from Europe we wouldn't be having this hearing.

—JOSE SERRANO, congressman
Hispanic Link Weekly Report, January 8, 1996

While Anglo California dreads and fears the immigrants, barricading itself in suburban gated communities as far as possible from inner cities teeming with "people of color," the newest Americans—documented or not—have assumed the optimism that once characterized the Golden State. They pool together resources to start up ma and pa businesses, they believe in the American Dream with almost evangelical fervor. They are pilgrims with a vision: a new Manifest Destiny, running from south to north.

—RUBÉN MARTÍNEZ, author
La Crisis: A Mexican Diary (a book in progress)

Immigration

Hey, you in the Saab, pull it over, Sven. Let's see your papers. You don't have any? I knew it! Green card? You don't have one? I knew it. Get out of your car. All right! I got another illegal alien. If the original Mexican border patrol had pulled over more Anglos, this would have still been Mexico.

—RICK NAJERA, comedian
The Pain of the Macho

LANGUAGE

She did not like the word "Chicano"—which, in her youth, in El Paso, Texas, had been a term of disapproval among Mexicans, and she did not refer to Los Angeles as "Ellay." "The city of angels!" she had said in awe when she arrived here from Texas with her two children—on an eerie day when Sant'Ana winds blew in from the hot desert and fire blazed along the horizon.

> —JOHN RECHY, author
> *The Miraculous Day of Amalia Gómez*

The struggle of every person who writes, of every true writer is primarily against the demon of that which resists being put into words. It is a struggle that spreads like an oil stain. Often, to surrender to the difficulty is to triumph, because the best text can sometimes be the one that allows words to have their own liberty.

> —LUISA VALENZUELA, author, educator
> "Writing with the Body," *The Writer on Her Work*

Language

We have let rhetoric do the job of poetry.
> —CHERRÍE MORAGA, author
> "La Guëra," *This Bridge Called My Back*

In this country, you cannot get works written in Spanish published. It's difficult. There are very few publishers who touch manuscripts written in Spanish. Then it would be difficult to market and distribute them.
> —RUDOLFO ANAYA, author
> *Interviews with Writers of the*
> *Post-Colonial World, 1992*

I think that incorporating the Spanish, for me, allows me to create new expressions in English—to say things in English that have never been said before. And I get to do that by translating literally. I love calling stories by Spanish expressions. I have this story called "Salvador, Late or Early." It's a nice title. It means "sooner or later," *tarde o temprano*, which literally translates as late or early. All of a sudden something happens to the English, something really new is happening, a new spice is added to the English language.

To me it's really fun to be doing that; to me it's like I've uncovered this whole mother lode that I haven't tapped into. All the expressions in Spanish when translated make English wonderful. I feel like I haven't finished playing around. I just feel so rich, as though you've given me all this new territory and said, "Okay, you can go in there and play."
> —SANDRA CISNEROS, author
> *Interviews with Writers of the*
> *Post-Colonial World, 1992*

They tell me that bilingualism is a characteristic of Chicano literature. . . . I could not say that, because to accept it would impose limitations on Chicano literature that in truth do not exist. The literature of the Chicano people is written in any standard or sub-standard dialect of Spanish or English. . . . The linguistic variants within Chicano literature simply reflect our linguistic reality, in spite of the purists.

—SERGIO ELIZONDO, professor, author

I think we're all [Chicano writers], in many ways, multilingual people. Most of the Chicanos in the Southwest are surely bilingual. So it comes naturally sometimes to shift back and forth. But it is more important to use the rhythms of Spanish in our work, the rhythms of Spanish in the Southwest, which is a unique blend of Spanish.

—RUDOLFO ANAYA, author
*Interviews with Writers of the
Post-Colonial World, 1992*

My grandfather used to call me seven tongues . . . because I talked so much.

—DOLORES HUERTA, activist
Notable Hispanic American Women

Today when the children in the elementary school I visited were playing the Mexican national anthem, "me emociono," it emotioned me, that's the only way I can phrase it. It "emotioned me"—it moved me—to hear them sing that Mexican national anthem.

—SANDRA CISNEROS, author
*Interviews with Writers of the
Post-Colonial World, 1992*

I'd probably be very unhappy were I to shut my mouth. I never think of what could happen [as a result of speaking out]. If I considered the consequences, I maybe wouldn't do many things.

—MARÍA CONCHITA ALONSO, actress, musician
Notable Hispanic American Women

We will never have "a" Chicano English or Spanish because of the regional differences. But I think that because of our bilingual history, we'll always be speaking a special kind of English and Spanish. What we do have to do is fight for the right to use those two languages in the way that it serves us. . . . I think the future of our language is where we claim our bilingualism for its unity.

—ANA CASTILLO, author
NuCity, July 1, 1993

Through language I was free. I could respond, escape, indulge, embrace or reject earth or the cosmos. I was launched on an endless journey without boundaries or rules, in which I could salvage the floating fragments of my past, or be born anew in the spontaneous ignition of understanding some heretofore concealed aspect of myself.

—JIMMY SANTIAGO BACA, author
"Working in the Dark," in volume 1 of
Hispanic Literature Criticism

Chicano literature's main characteristic is that it is a literature that is naturally at ease in the way that Chicanos express themselves, and that is a natural bilingualism, with the influence of English naturally predominant, as that is the language in which all Chicanos are educated. . . . Chicano literature is heavily spiced with *calo* [slang] and a sort of regionalism, and even ungrammatical standard expressions which give it flavor peculiar to Chicanos. To write using natural bilingual style is a very vivid affirmation that we are here, that we are alive and well, thinking and writing in both *idiomas* [languages], and that there are many like us out there in that mythical Aztlan who also think and talk and write as we do.

—ABELARDO DELGADO, educator

LITERATURE

Both technically and thematically Chicano literature is a revolutionary force in that it advocates a change not necessarily solicited, welcome, or wanted, by the dominant culture. Chicano literature is revolutionary in that it imposes itself forcefully rather than sits back for natural evolution to invite it in.

—ABELARDO DELGADO, educator

You also ask yourself—and this is really overwhelming—why write at all? In my case, I belong, body and soul and mind, to the so-called Third World where certain needs exist that are not at all literary.

—LUISA VALENZUELA, author, educator
"Writing with the Body," *The Writer on Her Work*

Some of our writings . . . ecologically speaking are so in tune with today and offer answers to our personal anxieties and fatigues, so that we can, in fact, say that Chicano

literature has in itself a curative effect for our present condition and despair. . . . The idea of poisoning water and
earth which give us life is certainly not in our culture.
While we acknowledge death as a very natural part of life,
we do not go around bending backwards to create it in
mass with nuclear plants. The curative effect of Chicano
literature frankly is that it offers us a bit of healthy insani-
ty, a valve to let out some of the frustrations of living as we
do in America, nay, in the whole world, today.

— ABELARDO DELGADO, educator

Chicano literature in the future will reflect a bicultural
condition. I do not believe there will be a disintegration of
either culture. . . . The Chicano's destiny is to create a new
literature. In the Chicano will be combined the best of
both cultures. He will be equally a homo emoere, a man
who feels, and a homo faber, a man who works. There will
be an ascending degree of integration of the cultures . . .
rather than the integration of the Chicano into one or the
other.

— ESTELA PORTILLO TRAMBLEY, author

The biggest milestone is that our barrios, our farmworkers, our pintos [brothers in prison], our still uneducated
and impoverished masses have accepted our work. How it
happened that Chicano literature emerged and that some
became interested in creating it and others in accepting it
and even demanding it is the question of the steady diet of
Cabacho [Anglo American] literature to which we had
been subjected for many years. The item suddenly appeared on the literature menu and people started to taste
it and order it again. It is obvious that certain conditions

had to exist; the question was one of an explosive readiness on everyone's part.

—ABELARDO DELGADO, educator

The irony of this [literature series, *Celebrando La Diferencia*] is that it started out as a little idea—a little idea!—that I had about how I could get kids to turn on to their culture without turning off to other cultures, and turn them on to it through literature. . . . There has been no bigger joy in my life, ever, than to have these little gang-bangers coming in and acting tough and walking out going "I got it."

—ELIZABETH PEÑA, actress
Hispanic, November 1994

The future [of literature] is bright. The de-emphasis will be on merely mirroring the cultural; in the sense of a representational or realistic mirroring of the culture, the trend is to a more personal work which will carry the culture in it, but will have a concern with experimentation, with style, and perhaps character.

—RUDOLFO ANAYA, author
Chicano Authors: Inquiry by Interview

The future of Chicano literature lies not in the de-emphasis of the distinctive characteristics, nor in its present distinctiveness. It will be the incorporation of still untapped, humanistic resources outside our barrio existentialism, its mythical font, or the romantic hold on "remembrances of things past." It lies in a convergence of truths that are universal, that places the Chicano within circumstances that focus the whole world.

—ESTELA PORTILLO TRAMBLEY, author

[My writing is] American literature and it is Chicano literature the way Faulkner's is Southern literature but eventually his is American. . . . It's not Mexican, for crying out loud, and it's certainly not Canadian. And it's not even regional because . . . the Mexican-American, Chicano, Hispanic experience is being felt all over now, in the United States.

—RUDOLFO ANAYA, author
Interviews with Writers of the
Post-Colonial World, 1992

Courses in Chicano literature, as other curricula in the emerging field of Chicano studies, when tolerated, are often treated as remnants of past political compromises and too frequently are perceived as tenuous academic endeavors. . . . [This has] kept at arm's length a wide range of comparative approaches and views that undoubtedly would have enriched the field.

—GUILLERMO E. HERNÁNDEZ, professor
Chicano Satire

LOS ANGELES

When I first came to Los Angeles, a young man looking for possible romance, the city met my glance with flattery. Los Angeles told me I was beautiful. Had I ever considered doing any modeling? No American city flattered the way Los Angeles flattered. I was 28 in L.A. I was 28 in this city for several years.

—RICHARD RODRIGUEZ, author
"The Flatterer," *Buzz* magazine,
January/February 1993

Poor pastless L.A., the city that demolished its Deco buildings, its Mission and Victorian, and Craftsman homes, in a delirious effort to create a future so far away from the East Coast—and its Southern, Mexican heritage. But the distance between Mexico and Los Angeles is growing shorter; the future is meeting its past.

—RUBÉN MARTÍNEZ, author
in *Saber Es Poder/Interventions*

I look at L.A. today and hardly recognize the city I first loved. But if any American city will heal the racial division of America, if any city will teach us what a multicultural America will look like, I think L.A. will be that city. The collision of tragedy with comedy here is creating a new world capital.
> —RICHARD RODRIGUEZ, author
> "The Flatterer," *Buzz* magazine, January/February 1993

It's very important for us to acknowledge the history of this place, its Spanish roots, the experience of the Chicano here, and how that translates into the condition of Los Angeles.
> —GUSTAVO LECLERC, architect, artist
> "Taming the Concrete Jungle," *Los Angeles Reader*, September 2, 1994

When I left L.A. a few years ago, it was because I spent too much time there looking at myself in various mirrors— the one in my car, the one in the gym, the one in my bathroom. The trouble with living in a city that flatters you as much as L.A. flatters you is that you end up in a mirror.
> —RICHARD RODRIGUEZ, author
> "The Flatterer," *Buzz* magazine, January/February 1993

[On California:]
A society in which a sense of history is continually sacrificed to a dream of the future.
> —A. ALVAREZ, journalist
> *Observer*, October 21, 1979

L.A. heartbreak: The city makes me feel old. The mistake of seeing an old lover?

—Richard Rodriguez, author
"The Flatterer," *Buzz* magazine,
January/February 1993

MANHOOD

I'm sorry, but I can't play a macho tonight. My therapist has warned me not to play a macho. He feels it would be very dangerous because I have worked very hard to get rid of the macho and I just don't want to regress. I hate the word macho. I prefer the more politically correct term, Latino males with strong opinions.

—RICK NAJERA, comedian
The Pain of the Macho

These boys on the street, they have nothing, no one to look up to. When we have men who will help our young males make the rite of passage into manhood, they will feel like men—and they will feel good. They won't have to search out for manhood among their peers who hand them guns.

—EDWARD JAMES OLMOS, actor
Los Angeles Times, May 10, 1992

Manhood

To be a man is to suffer for others. God help us be men!
>—CÉSAR CHÁVEZ, activist
>> statement on the conclusion of a twenty-five-day
>> fast for nonviolence, read to eight thousand
>> farmworkers gathered in Delano, California, on
>> Sunday, March 10, 1968

Eddie blew his head off.
Playing chicken
with his brother. Para proof
he was a man . . .
>—JIMMY SANTIAGO BACA, author
>> "Martin and Meditations on the South Valley,"
>> in volume 1 of *Hispanic Literature Criticism*

MEXICO

A cruel fantasy [Mexico as Oz]: the history of Mexico was a history of crushing defeats, whereas I lived in a world, that of my D.C. public school, which celebrated victories, one victory after another, from Yorktown to New Orleans to Chapultepec to Appomattox to San Juan Hill to Belleau Wood: had this nation ever known defeat? Sometimes the names of United States victories were the same as the names of Mexico's defeats and humiliations: Monterrey. Veracruz. Chapultepec. Indeed: from the Halls of Montezuma to the shores of Tripoli.

At home, my father made me read Mexican history, study Mexican geography, and understand the names, the dreams and defeats of Mexico: a nonexistent country, I then thought, invented by my father to nourish my infant imagination with yet another marvelous fiction: a land of Oz with a green cactus road, a landscape and a soul so different from those of the United States that they seemed a fantasy.

Mexico

To the south, sad songs, sweet nostalgia, impossible desires. To the north, self-confidence, faith in progress, boundless optimism. Mexico, the imaginary country [to Fuentes's youthful perception], dreamed of a painful past; the United States, the real country, dreamed of a happy future.

> —CARLOS FUENTES, author
> "How I Started to Write," *The Graywolf Annual Five: Multi-Cultural Literacy*

MUSIC

I was born gifted. I can speak of my gifts with little or no modesty, but with tremendous gratitude, precisely because they are gifts, and not things which I created, or actions about which I might be proud.

—Joan Baez, musician, activist
And a Voice to Sing With

To be a musician you have to be a slave to the instrument. You cannot wing things. . . . Music exists in the moment only, so everything must be exactly right.

—Marta Istomin, artistic director
Washingtonian, December 1987

The pulse of Latin music is beating more vigorously than at any time in the music's long and distinguished history, from clubs in East Los Angeles, where dancers and serious listeners respond enthusiastically as conquero Poncho Sanchez and his octet carry on a tradition pioneered half a century ago by Machito and Puente, to the urban heart of the hip-hop culture, where groups like the Barrio Boyzz are igniting genuine excitement with their sleek blend of bicultural influences.

—MARK HOLSTON, journalist
Hispanic, December 1992

[Speaking of musician Tish Hinojosa:]
Her art is deeply rooted in the traditions of her ancestors. In her songs, the spirit of our people is given voice.

—AMÉRICO PAREDES, professor
Hispanic, January/February 1994

I love the music of the traditional aspect of our community. Conjunto music, the ballads, and the romantic singer/songwriter songs—the older music from Mexico that my parents like a lot—made a very positive impression. There's a sense of the guitar and the voice. I guess it ties in the folk element, which really excites me.

—TISH HINOJOSA, musician
Hispanic, January/February 1994

Throughout the United States, a growing number of Hispanic artists are stepping out of the background onto center stage and finding success with multicultural audiences that were beyond their grasp just a few years ago. The trend cuts across stylistic lines and is demolishing long-held stereotypes about Latino musicians and performers in the United States.

—MARK HOLSTON, journalist
Hispanic, December 1992

We've been crossing over for years. Xavier Cougat was the first to really cross over from the strictly Spanish-speaking audience. And even the earliest rock was strongly influenced by Latin forms.

—TONY SABOURNIN, Latin music authority
Hispanic, December 1992

Today, I'm performing places we've never been to before, like Cheyenne, Wyoming, and Winnipeg, Manitoba, where not many people understand Spanish, but they love the music. . . . You see, instrumental music has no language problem. I get a lot of airplay on radio because my music can help bridge the gap to Spanish-language music. And people love the rhythm. They love to dance to it.

—TITO PUENTE, musician
Hispanic, December 1992

Today, with [Tito Puente's] 102nd album in the stores and on the airwaves, a new concert-length video in circulation, and non-stop touring a daily fact of life, the indefatigable percussionist is as hot a commodity as he was when he first captured the public's imagination in the early 1950s.

—MARK HOLSTON, journalist
Hispanic, December 1992

That's one reason why the kids are into [rap music]. It's because their parents aren't. It's that simple. Their parents aren't. It's that simple. The parents are not into the violence of it, the rage of it.

—KID FROST (Arturo Molina), musician
Hispanic, January/February 1993

Music

[Commenting on "Repeticiones," a musical style of reciting and then translating lyrics from one language into another while maintaining the same rhyme and meter:]

It's too tricky for most. For me it comes naturally, and picking up on the meanings of foreign words seems to come naturally to listeners this way. It's amazing how language barriers are bulldozed when people hear my songs. I am the maestro, the inventor, the teacher.

—MELLOW MAN ACE (Ulpiano Reyes), musician
Hispanic, January/February 1993

I prefer to call my music "Positive Rap," but it does have a Christian message. I like to remind church-going people about important things, like not prejudging new members or being hypocritical.

—M.C. GEEGEE (Genie Rodriguez), musician
Hispanic, January/February 1993

Like popular music, the world of Hispanic rap boasts the profound and the superficial, the daring and the reserved, the hot and the cool. Once exclusively an outsider's music, rap is now so much a part of the mainstream that even establishment entertainers, such as Spanish crooner Raphael, now consider it all but obligatory to include a taste of rap on their new recordings.

—MARK HOLSTON, journalist
Hispanic, January/February 1993

[My husband, Pablo Casals] used to say that music, each note, was like nature, always different. You would never see the sun rise the same way.
—MARTA ISTOMIN, artistic director
Washingtonian, December 1987

I just feel great that people are enjoying the music— jumping to it, dancing to it, even in places where they don't understand a word of the language. . . . In the year 2000, we'll be doing a lot more lyrics in English, and we'll see a lot of hip-hop kids coming back to salsa. . . . There's no question about it. When we get to the year 2000, we'll still be swingin'. The beat will be stronger than ever.
—RALPH MERCADO, producer
Hispanic, December 1992

Rap's the voice and expression of the street. There's got to be negative; there's got to be positive. Gotta be up, down, yin and yang. Day and night. It all fits together.
—KID FROST, musician
Hispanic, January/February 1993

Salsa music is usually for escape and fun for the working class. For the first time in a dance format, short stories were offered and comment of issues of general interest. I took barrio issues and put them in general context.
—RUBÉN BLADES, actor
Rising Voices: Profiles in Leadership

It's the Anglos at the record companies who are seeing the Mexican culture that they want to see. When I see that, I automatically want to give more and show another facet. I guess that's always been my mission and purpose, and, in fact, that's what has kept me on the fringes of not being in the mainstream of any one of these specific styles for the last fifteen years of my life.

—Tish Hinojosa, musician
Hispanic, January/February 1994

We're trying to do something to show these kids there is a better way, an alternative, and a way to make something out of their lives. I'm making people listen and realize that we have a problem, and that they face it and address it. If we can reach one kid out there, and he puts a gun down and says, "I ain't gonna kill this guy—I'm gonna listen to Frost, you know, there's no sunshine in jail"—if we can do that, then it's worked.

—Kid Frost, musician
Hispanic, January/February 1993

I'd lock myself up in my room with my guitar. I wouldn't cry. I was afraid if I let go just a little bit, it would all go. I would sing for hours by myself. . . . It was my way of crying.

—Gloria Estefan, musician
Rolling Stone, June 14, 1990

When I step up to the microphone I feel like it's "Round One." I'm jumpin' into the ring and I gotta do my job and say what I say the hardest way I can, in the toughest manner. I try to communicate to the mentality of the young Chicano street warrior. I want to be a conscience for the kids who don't have any. If people listen closely to my records, they will find that the lyric content is straight up against gang violence and dedicated to kicking the reality of the streets.

—KID FROST, musician
The Hispanic Reporter, August 1994

NONVIOLENCE

I have been true to the principles of nonviolence, developing a stronger and stronger aversion to the ideologies of both the far right and the far left and a deeper sense of rage and sorrow over the suffering they continue to produce all over the world.

—JOAN BAEZ, musician, activist
And a Voice to Sing With

If you win non-violently, then you have a double victory, you have not only won your fight, but you remain free.

—CÉSAR CHÁVEZ, activist
Roots of Greatness: The 1995 Mexican American Historical Calendar

No child I've ever known has come out of his mother's womb with a pistol in his hand.

—EDWARD JAMES OLMOS
Press-Telegram, March 12, 1995

I think we [the United Farm Workers] brought to the world, the United States, anyway, the whole idea of boycotting as a nonviolent tactic. I think we showed the world that nonviolence can work to make social change . . . I think we have laid a pattern of how farm workers are eventually going to get out of their bondage.

—DOLORES HUERTA, activist
Notable Hispanic American Women

POLITICS

Whereas Barbra Streisand, Charlton Heston, even Arnold Schwarzenegger [who is foreign born] conduct fundraisers and proudly identify themselves with their candidates of choice, we don't hear of Hispanic celebrities openly supporting their preferred candidates.

—ELENA KELLNER, journalist
Hispanic, October 1993

Certain Chicanos will say to me, "Why don't you write more about politics? You're not really writing about *la causa*." The funny thing is the laborers are very much aware that even talking about the working class is extremely "cause"—it's the oldest, most radical cause in this country. It's a dangerous subject. A lot of people don't see that. And there's nothing I can say. If you don't get it, you don't get it.

—DAGOBERTO GILB, author
Los Angeles Times Magazine, November 12, 1995

We have numbers on our side. Already we are an economic power, and a growing one. Someday, everyone will realize it.

—RAÚL JULIA, actor
Hispanic Hollywood

In front of a packed church, [Father Luis Olivares] presented [INS regional director Harold] Ezell with a letter that promised that families would not be separated in the amnesty process and asked him to sign it. "He said, 'This is a bunch of crap,' and stomped out in a rage," Olivares once told me, laughing mischievously.

—RUBÉN MARTÍNEZ, journalist
LA Weekly, April 2–8, 1993

Our real leaders, that is, people who actually run the country, are rarely inspirational enough to satisfy our need for romantic self-identity.

—RUBÉN SALAZAR, journalist
Los Angeles Times, July 17, 1970

What regrets I have about being party to killing and maiming thousands of Japanese civilians this morning are tempered with the hope that this terrible weapon we have created may bring the countries of the world together and prevent further wars.

—LUIS ALVAREZ, physicist
from a letter to his four-year-old son upon
the bombing of Hiroshima, August 6, 1945

Many consider the 1950s as the decade in which the battle for civil rights was fought, and the 1960s and 1970s as the time when civil rights were won. If the current political trend continues, the 1990s will be remembered as the decade in which certain segments of the population were not simply deprived of their civil or human rights, but were attacked by policies of "anti-rights."

> —ROBERTO RODRIGUEZ and PATRISIA GONZALES, authors
> *Latino Spectrum*

The Lord's command is clear. In the Book of Leviticus, God says, "When aliens reside with you in your land . . . you shall treat them no differently than the natives born among you." In light of the Gospel call to justice, we find ourselves unable to comply with the current regulations [on Salvadoran refugees].

> —FATHER LUIS OLIVARES, pastor
> advocating the Sanctuary movement, 1985

Hispanics in the City of New York, as well as in the rest of the country, are becoming a force that others have to reckon with. As long as we have people such as ourselves who are given an opportunity to assume responsibility in government and in the private sector, we can begin to prove that we can do just as well as anybody else.

> —MIGUEL O. MARTÍNEZ, artist
> *Portraits*

Predictions over the amount of political, cultural and economic power Latinos will wield in this country vary about as much as seismologists' forecasts for when the Big One will hit California, but one thing is certain: both will occur, and everyone wants to be prepared.

—SANDRA HERNANDEZ, journalist
LA Weekly, November 3–9, 1995

I don't know what my politics are, except that my stories tell it to you. I can't give it to you as an -ism or an -ist.
—SANDRA CISNEROS, author
Interviews with Writers of the Post-Colonial World, 1992

The revolution begins at home.

—CHERRÍE MORAGA and GLORIA ANZALDÚA, authors
This Bridge Called My Back

Artists make their greatest political statement with their art.

—ANTONIO MEJÍAS-RENTAS, editor
Hispanic, October 1993

I hope that being the first woman and minority Surgeon General since the post came into being—and the visibility that the post confers—enables me to reach many individuals with my message of empowerment for women, children and minorities.

—ANTONÍA NOVELLO, former Surgeon General
Hispanic, January/February 1990

Now, let's take that common denominator, that organizing tool of nationalism and utilize it against the system. Let's use it to work against the two parties that I say are like an animal with two heads eating at the same trough, that sits on the same board of directors of the banks and corporations, that shares in the same industries that makes dollars and profits off wars. To fight this thing you look for the tools. . . . Now what are the tools? We said nationalism, which means that we have to be able to identify with our past and understand our past in order that we can dedicate ourselves to the future. . . . And we have to understand what humanism really is. We can tie the cultural thing into it, but we also have to tie in the economic and political. We tie these things together and we start to use the common denominator of nationalism. . . . We start to consider ourselves a nation.

—RODOLFO "CORKY" GONZÁLES, activist
Famous Mexican-Americans

It's our own fault, not the gringos'. We don't have a Latino leader on a national scale. And more importantly, we continue to behave like warring tribes. Cubans don't get along with Puerto Ricans. Mexicans don't get along with Central Americans. Mexican Americans don't understand South Americans. It's crazy.

—RUBÉN BLADES, actor
Hispanic, October 1993

I don't see Hispanic celebrities vocally or visibly out there supporting candidates. While Edward James Olmos and a

few others get involved, we don't have the clout or the visibility to make a dent in the Washington political scene.
—LUIS REYES, publicist
Hispanic, October 1993

Hopefully, someday it will be possible to see a Latino or a Latina become President. But I'm not that person. I don't think it's something that's going to happen in my lifetime.
—HENRY CISNEROS, public official
Los Angeles Times Magazine, February 27, 1994

If you are ready to criticize a system, be equally prepared to offer assistance to improve it.
—ARMANDO SANCHEZ, educator

Increased funding for transportation creates jobs both directly at the construction site or vehicle manufacturer and indirectly through increased orders for materials and equipment to support transportation improvements.
—FEDERICO PEÑA, Secretary of Transportation
Hispanic, June 1993

Now Amalia recognized the family, from television news. He was a político, a powerful city politician who constantly proclaimed his "Chicano heritage" and wept openly on American holidays while holding his hand over his heart. Whether his wife was Mexican or not, her hair was bleached, and their children were chattering in English. My children learned Spanish and English, I saw to it, Amalia thought.
—JOHN RECHY, author
The Miraculous Day of Amalia Gómez

Politics

The Democrats can't take the Latino vote for granted. We must make them accountable to our issues.
—LINDA CHÁVEZ-THOMPSON, labor official
Hispanic Link Weekly Report, January 8, 1996

The only reason sanctuary exists is because neither the laws nor the policy of a given country is fulfilling their obligation under international law, and that's really the case here in the United States in regard to political refugees.
—FATHER LUIS OLIVARES, pastor
El Popo, Spring 1988

[Commenting on the 1996 presidential race:]
We have the mass and numbers in these key states [California, Texas, Illinois, New York, New Jersey, and Florida]. We are the swing vote.
—RAÚL YZAGUIRRE, public official
Hispanic Link Weekly Report, January 8, 1996

Politically, I believe that our American system works as long as you participate in it. You must vote and make your voice heard. Otherwise you will be left out.
—MARI-LUCI JARAMILLO, educator, diplomat
Notable Hispanic American Women

I haven't seen any evidence of any sizable connection between Washington and Hispanic actors.
—RODOLFO O. DE LA GARZA, professor
Hispanic, October 1993

I was not rich and had never participated in party politics, two things I thought were essential to political appointments.

—MARI-LUCI JARAMILLO, educator, diplomat
Notable Hispanic American Women

POVERTY

The statement "They're so poor they can't afford to contribute to the group" is a great cop-out. You don't organize people by being afraid of them. In fact, at the very beginning of the organizing drive, we looked for the worst homes in the barrios where there were a lot of dogs and kids outside. And we went in and asked for a handout. Inevitably, they gave us food. Then they took a collection and gave us money for gas. They opened their homes and they gave us their hearts.

—CÉSAR CHÁVEZ, activist

There is a side of poverty, exacerbated by race, that is much more difficult to understand. It is subtle yet oppressive. It is communicated by stares, gestures, and tone. Unless you've been there, you can't possibly understand.

—JOSEPH TOVARES, journalist
Hispanic, May 1995

In this country, lesbianism is a poverty—as is being brown, as is being a woman, as is being just plain poor. The danger lies in ranking the oppressions.
>   —CHERRÍE MORAGA, author
>   "La Guëra," *This Bridge Called My Back*

There is a point at which you see the development of a permanent underclass, and that's frightening. The tradition of the immigrant rising up through work is only partly true. So an anger sets in. In the film [*Mi Familia*], the oppression becomes very hard to bear for members of the family. That reality of Los Angeles—a divided city—is still there.
>   —GREGORY NAVA, filmmaker
>   *Los Angeles Times Magazine*, May 1995

RELIGION

I revel in my Catholicism. I find it a great source of energy and strength and imagination, because I've always used it. You try to use the positive aspects of that upbringing. . . . You have to take these things tongue-in-cheek. I'm a happy Catholic, what can I say.

—DENISE CHÁVEZ, educator, author
NuCity, August 29–September 4, 1994

There was a time when being Hispanic and being Catholic were synonymous. Such a familiar correlation can no longer be made. Thousands of Hispanics are now members of other religious institutions. . . . Such numbers, unfortunately, are more than converts to these groups but defections of former Roman Catholic Hispanics to institutions in which they have found a home.

—ALEX GARCÍA-RIVERA, pastor
U.S. Catholic, July 1994

Given the relative weakness of institutionalized religion that struggles to finance parishes and schools, the cohesiveness of Latinos as a major constituency of American religion is likely to increase, not diminish.
—Antónío Stevens-Arroyo, educator
Program for the Analysis of Religion Among Latinos
Christian Century, April 6, 1994

We Latinos weren't personally involved in the historic denominational splits, so we aren't invested in maintaining them. Because Anglo evangelicals define themselves in contrast to liberals and fundamentalists, they have a much more difficult time at ecumenism. For us, since liberalism was never really an issue in our churches, we define ourselves in contrast to nonbelievers and Catholics, making ecumenism among Protestants easier.
—Justo L. Gonzalez, director
Christianity Today, February 6, 1995

. . . little by little, I began to see that maybe one person's reality was, indeed, another's fantasy—especially if their childhood perceptions of the world were so different. I came to understand why my father had always told me that it was easy to call another's religion superstition.
—Victor Villaseñor, author
Rain of Gold

In many ways, Latino evangelicos can be more dogmatic about denominational differences than Anglo Christians. Having been a religious people all along and growing up in the Catholic church, the conversion experience to whatever Protestant denomination becomes especially

significant. For those who say "Here is where I found God!" it's difficult not to make their experience normative.
—JESSE MIRANDA, educator
Christianity Today, February 6, 1995

Mexicans have always asked themselves why a people so close to God should be so close to the United States.
—CARLOS FUENTES, author
W, October 29, 1976

The real challenge for current religious leadership is to open the door to ways the Hispanic reality can enrich the religious experience of all Americans and at the same time . . . encourage unique religious expressions among the diverse groups of people who call themselves Latinos.
—KENNETH B. BEDELL, author
Christian Century, April 6, 1994

SPORTS

After all these years it's still embarrassing for me to play on the American golf tour. Like the time I asked my caddie for a sand wedge and he comes back 10 minutes later with a ham on rye.

—CHICHI RODRÍGUEZ, golfer
Sports Illustrated, March 8, 1976

If you don't throw it, they can't catch it

—LEFTY GOMEZ, baseball player
Washingtonian, November 1979

Baseball has been a sport in which Hispanics have achieved tremendous success. And in that regard, many role models and outstanding individuals have emerged as players. So as a Hispanic, this sport was attractive to me in terms of the kinds of excellence that Hispanics have achieved. It was a natural evolution for me as a business-person to want to look at being a part of ownership.

—Linda Alvarado, businesswoman
Hispanic, April 1993

STEREOTYPES

I've had it with stereotypes, with scripts about the poor, struggling Chicano people of the barrio.... Some say I've been lucky. I have worked. I played cocaine dealers, a poor barrio mother, a decent but poor Chicano girlfriend of a poor, bad and uneducated Chicano boxer, a Tijuana hooker, a poor Mexican village girl, a homeless Tijuana beggar woman, and a suffering barrio mother of a juvenile gang member.... All poor, all uneducated, and most of them named Maria.

—Dyana Ortelli, actress
Hispanic Hollywood

[Hispanics] have very little representation in the United States, so whoever is up there at the moment becomes representative of the whole Latin experience. That would be impossible because we are not monolithic.

—John Leguizamo, actor
Hispanic, March 1992

Stereotypes

Badges? We ain't got no badges. We don't need no badges. I don't have to show you any stinking badges.
—ALFONSO BEDOYA, actor
in *The Treasure of the Sierra Madre*

[*Spic-O-Rama*] is my little tunnel vision of the Latin experience and there's a lot of wannabe, middle-class, intellectual, quasi-pseudo people who are the forefront elitist of the Latin world up there, and they don't want to be portrayed that way.
—JOHN LEGUIZAMO, actor
Hispanic, March 1992

[The image of the philandering Latin lover with an irrepressible libido] is largely a stereotype, a stereotype that is sometimes encouraged by the Latino male himself. There is a lot of exaggeration about that sort of thing.
—RUDY ZEA, psychologist
Hispanic, January–February 1995

STORYTELLING

I hope you will go out and let stories happen to you, and that you will work them, water them with your blood and tears and your laughter till they bloom, till you yourself burst into bloom. Then you will see what medicine they make, and where and when to apply them. That is the work. The only work.

—CLARISSA PINKOLA ESTES, author
Women Who Run with the Wolves

He was a great storyteller and without much effort Cartagena was transported to far-off places; Raymond's mesmerizing voice weaving incredible tales set in bazaars in North Africa; his language fluid and rich, filled with foreign words which Cartagena was certain were being pronounced exactly as they were meant to be, this later proven by listening to him speak a dozen languages fluently.

—ED VEGA, author
"An Apology to the Moon Furies,"
Hispanics in the United States

In the ethno-poetics and performance of the shaman, my people, the Indians, did not split the artistic from the functional, the sacred from the secular, art from everyday life. The religious, social, and aesthetic purposes of art were all intertwined. Before the Conquest, poets gathered to play music, dance, sing, and read poetry in open-air places around the Xochicuahuitl, el Arbol Florido, Tree-in-Flower.

. . . The ability of story (prose and poetry) to transform the storyteller and the listener into something or someone else is shamanistic. The writer, as shape-changer, is a nahual, a shaman.

—GLORIA ANZALDÚA, author
"Tlilli, Tlapalli: The Path of the
Red and Black Ink"

I think that most people like to daydream about the times when they were young and what storytelling did for them. I think it's a very rewarding experience. Even the older people like storytelling. They come in and they laugh and they play. It's like they're little children all over again.

—PAULETTE ATENCIO, author
Notable Hispanic American Women

My "stories" are acts encapsulated in time, "enacted" every time they are spoken aloud or read silently. I like to think of them as performances and not as inert and "dead" objects. . . . The work manifests the same needs as a person, it needs to be "fed," *la tengo que bañar y vestir.*

—GLORIA ANZALDÚA, author
"Tlilli, Tlapalli: The Path of the
Red and Black Ink"

The world is changing so much; everybody is in a hurry and television has to do the entertaining or little children have to entertain themselves. When we were growing up it wasn't like our parents had to get after us or hit us, it was through their storytelling, it set an example. Every story has a moral and there is always a lesson to be learned from it.

—PAULETTE ATENCIO, author
Notable Hispanic American Women

I was familiar with *cuentos*—my grandmother told stories like the one about her getting on top of the roof while down below rabid coyotes were ravaging the place and wanting to get at her. My father told stories about a phantom giant dog that appeared out of nowhere and sped along the side of the pickup no matter how fast he was driving.

Nudge a Mexican and she or he will break out with a story.

—GLORIA ANZALDÚA, author
"Tlilli, Tlapalli: The Path of the
Red and Black Ink"

[*La invitada*, a chair provided for unexpected guests] is always present at storytelling. Sometime during a telling the soul of one or more of the audience comes and sits there, for it has a need. Although I may have a whole evening of material prepared, I often change it to mend or play with the spirit that comes to the empty chair. The guest always speaks to the needs of all.

—CLARISSA PINKOLA ESTES, author
Women Who Run with the Wolves

SURVIVAL

The poor who migrate into a richer nation do not pose a threat to the local culture. In fact, the opposite is true. The threat is to their own self-image and cultural identity.

—FATHER VIRGIL P. ELIZONDO, pastor
"The Future Is Mestizo: Life Where Cultures Meet,"
Barrios and Borderlands

My art, work, family and friends, my son Gabe, and a curious relationship with God remain the sustaining forces of my life.

—JOAN BAEZ, musician, activist
And a Voice to Sing With

Loneliness: It is a continual, almost palpable quality which the country gives off like a heat shimmer. It is no less present in the utter separateness and indifference of city life, the blank size of the buildings, the self-sufficiency

of the different ethnic ghettoes, than in the deserts and mountains of the Southwest.
—A. ALVAREZ, journalist
"American Afterthoughts," *Encounter*, June 1965

I know all about loneliness—only I don't whine about it.
—ANTHONY QUINN, actor
in *Lust for Life*

I made strength from everything that had happened to me, so that in the end even the final tragedy could not defeat me. And that is what Ultima tried to teach me, that the tragic consequences of life can be overcome by the magical strength that resides in the human heart.
—RUDOLFO ANAYA, author
Bless Me, Ultima

The weeks of unemployment and hard knocks turned into months. I continued to find two or three days of work here and there. And I continued to be thrown out when I rebelled at the ill treatment, overwork and insults. I kept pounding the streets looking for a place where they would treat me half decently. . . . I remember the worn out shoes I bought in a secondhand store on Myrtle Avenue at the corner of Adams Street. The round holes in the soles that I tried to cover with pieces of carton were no match for the frigid knives of the unrelenting snow.
—JESÚS COLÓN, author, journalist
A Puerto Rican in New York

When we are not physically starving, we have the luxury to realize psychic and emotional starvation.
>   —CHERRÍE MORAGA, author
>   "La Güera," *This Bridge Called My Back*

Living on borders and in margins, keeping intact one's shifting and multiple identity and integrity, is like trying to swim in a new element, an "alien" element.
>   —GLORIA ANZALDÚA, author
>   *Borderlands/La Frontera: The New Mestiza*

When they surrounded the house,
Cortez suddenly appeared before them,
"You will take me if I'm willing,
But not any other way."
>   —AMÉRICO PAREDES, professor
>   *The Ballad of Gregorio Cortéz* (screenplay)

VALUES

You don't get to choose how you're going to die. Or when. You can only decide how you're going to live. Now.
—JOAN BAEZ, musician, activist
Daybreak

When we are really honest with ourselves we must admit that our lives are all that really belong to us. So, it is how we use our lives that determines what kind of men we are. It is my deepest belief that only by giving our lives do we find life. I am convinced that the truest act of courage, the strongest act of manliness is to sacrifice for others in a totally nonviolent struggle for justice.
—CÉSAR CHÁVEZ, activist
statement on the conclusion of a twenty-five-day fast for nonviolence, read to eight thousand farmworkers gathered in Delano, California, on Sunday, March 10, 1968

Values

I am ready to work
all I ask is that I don't starve,
that I don't fail at being a good man,
that things go good for me,
that I meet a woman who will love me deeply,
that I meet strong spiritual brothers and sisters,
and that I have healthy children.
—JIMMY SANTIAGO BACA, author
"Martin and Meditations on the South Valley,"
in volume 1 of *Hispanic Literature Criticism*

When I got off the plane [in Puerto Rico], kids from my mother's school lined both sides of the road handing me flowers. . . . I went to the VA hospital to speak. When the veterans saw my gold [Vice Admiral in Public Health Service] braid, they all stood and saluted. . . . For these people, for women, I have to be good as a doctor, I have to be good as a Surgeon General, I have to be everything.
—ANTONÍA NOVELLO, former Surgeon General
Washington Post, May 8, 1990

I change myself, I change the world.
—GLORIA ANZALDÚA, author
Borderlands/La Frontera: The New Mestiza

I want the good things that I have done to outweigh the bad. I believe that only then will I find beautiful things waiting at the end of the rainbow.
—PAULETTE ATENCIO, author
Notable Hispanic American Women

I want to be able to say in the last four seconds of my life that I tried to do my best. Only then will I smile. Only then will I be at peace with myself.

—RUBÉN BLADES, actor
Rising Voices: Profiles in Leadership

I tell the kids, "I'm your worst nightmare, because I know all the excuses. I've had to learn the first rule: forgive yourself. It's a nightmare to think of all the things you do to hurt yourself. But you can't make excuses. You can't say, 'If only things had been different.' Not everyone can do it. But you must *try* not to use the excuse."

—EDWARD JAMES OLMOS, actor
Los Angeles Magazine, April 1993

I learned there is no substitute for persistence. It overrides everything.

—ANDY GARCÍA, actor
Rising Voices: Profiles in Leadership

Take care of your family first. But then reach out to your neighbor, your block, your city, your country. Everybody wants change, but they want it to come by way of somebody else. Hey, not in the '90s. If you wait for the government, you'll wait a long time.

—EDWARD JAMES OLMOS, actor
Los Angeles Magazine, April 1993

Values

The ads have youth believing that instead of getting up early, exercising, going to school, playing a sport or learning to be a team player, all they have to do to be fit is learn to drink the right alcohol.

—ANTONÍA NOVELLO, former Surgeon General

History has placed us in a difficult situation. We have to be prepared to compete. We have to deal with the traditional things that are holding us back. If we do not prepare ourselves for a high level, we cannot fit into this society.

—RAMONA SALGADO, professor
Portraits

In the land of opportunity, only those who don't see it are doomed to mediocrity.

—FRANSISCO AVELAR, educator

You become a true caring physician when you're able to share the pain.

—ANTONÍA NOVELLO, former Surgeon General
Glamour, August 1990

When power is used as a means to control other people and their destinies, I think that is a sin.

—FATHER LUIS OLIVARES, pastor
LA Weekly, September 6–12, 1991

I wasn't allowed to work until I graduated from medical school because my mother felt that once I earned money I might be sidetracked by material rewards before I got to my real work.

—ANTONÍA NOVELLO, former Surgeon General
Glamour, August 1990

Courage is the atom of change.

—BETTINA R. FLORES, author
Chiquita's Cocoon

But you can't stop progress! I mean, after you have the computer, you can't go back to the abacus. Don't you want things to change?

—DOLORES PRIDA, author
"Savings," *Barrios and Borderlands*

If you believe in yourself, that means you're thinking positively, and you'll make it; you're gonna do it! But if you have a negative image about yourself, you'll really kill yourself. One of the greatest things you have in life is that no one has the authority to tell you what you want to be. You're the one who'll decide what you want to be. Respect yourself and respect the integrity of others as well. The greatest thing you have is your self image, a positive opinion of yourself. You must never let anyone take it from you.

—JAIME ESCALANTE, educator
Technos, Spring 1993

Values

We all start out with no discipline, no patience, no perseverance, no determination. We all start out at zero. People say, "You have talent." No, the gift is to realize that we all start out even. Whether we messed up or put our best foot forward, with these four qualities, we take care of our mental, physical and spiritual health each day. Am I the best in the world? No. The question is: Am I the best I can be?

—EDWARD JAMES OLMOS, actor
Los Angeles Times, September 1, 1991

With *ganas* (desire) anybody can do it. Believe in yourself, because I know you can do it. You have proven it to me.

—JAIME ESCALANTE, educator
Monterey Pare Progress, September 2, 1991

Latinos tend to think "if I do this, how will it affect others?" We don't think "me first and to hell with everyone else." We may decide later to do it anyway, but we first consider the impact on others.

—DAVID HAYES-BAUTISTA, editor
Rising Voices: Profiles in Leadership

It was very easy to rationalize that [formerly high-flying] way of life as something I have to do to serve the order. It doesn't enter your mind that you've become more concerned with the stock market than with real people until you actually come in contact again with the disadvantaged and those who are working so hard on their behalf.

—FATHER LUIS OLIVARES, pastor
LA Weekly, September 6–12, 1991

It is the child who produces the future, it is the child who produces the hope. So if the child is not put first, you have no dreams. But that isn't what's happening. If we did put the child first, every child would learn how to read and write. There would be no illiteracy. And then people say, "We give them the opportunity, but the families have broken down." It's true. But why? It's because the dollar has become the single most powerful motivating factor in our society.

—EDWARD JAMES OLMOS, actor
Los Angeles Magazine, April 1993

[L]ook for your passion and follow it, come what may, but do it from a Latino perspective, where you are guided by the effect of what you do on your family and on your community. Being Latino is emotional, is spiritual, and to me it means moral structure: what is good, what is right, what is justice. All this will become more important as we go through some tough times ahead. We need to build on that.

—DAVID HAYES-BAUTISTA, editor
Rising Voices: Profiles in Leadership

If you haven't forgiven yourself something, how can you forgive others?

—DOLORES HUERTA, activist
in Barbara L. Baer, "Stopping Traffic,
One Woman's Cause," *The Progressive*

WOMEN

Today, Hispanic women continue to preserve their culture and family unity while advancing their own careers. Often they step into the public arena to address social and political issues to ensure a brighter future for generations to follow.

—ILEANA ROS-LEHTINEN, congresswoman
Rising Voices: Profiles in Leadership

But those whose vision of feminism extends beyond career trajectories to the search for wholeness inextricably tied to justice need to say there is another perspective on citizenship, valor, and patriotism.

—ANNETTE FUENTES, author
The Nation, October 1991

Men and women exist in the same time and place, but in different dimensions.

—ISABEL ALLENDE, author
El plan infinito

A married Latina who has aspired to the rank of Christ is called La Santita. We all know her, don't we? She's the Super-Latina whom everyone pretends to admire. She's the one who holds the family together, keeps order and peace, waits on her husband and family hand and foot twenty-four hours a day and always excuses her husband's behavior, even when he beats her or blows the family paycheck. And she never complains.

—BETTINA R. FLORES, author
Chiquita's Cocoon

Traditional psychology is often spare or entirely silent about deeper issues important to women; the archetypal, the intuitive, the sexual and cyclical, the ages of women, a woman's way, a woman's knowing, her creative fire. This is what has motivated my work on the Wild Woman archetype for the better part of two decades.

—CLARISSA PINKOLA ESTES, author
Women Who Run with the Wolves

When a Latina breaks away from the home roost, she's labeled a loose woman rather than someone seeking independence and space in which to grow.

—BETTINA R. FLORES, author
Chiquita's Cocoon

Always there is the echo of the young girl in the oldest of women, in small wrists encased in bulky flesh, in the brightest of eyes surrounded by wrinkles.

—DENISE CHÁVEZ, educator, author
The Last of the Menu Girls

"You are too intelligent to be beautiful" is what many of us have been told at some time by a man we've loved. Or, supposing literature is your profession: "You are too intelligent to be a good writer." Contrasting, of course, that ugly, masculine thing which is intelligence with female intuition.

. . . But those marks were made on young and tender skin, and from that moment on, one will always have a feeling of inadequacy.

> —LUISA VALENZUELA, author, educator
> "Writing with the Body," *The Writer on Her Work*

What had been unthinkable 20 years ago and unattainable 10 years ago—the full integration of women into the voluntary military service—happened last summer when the Senate and the House voted to eliminate regulations that prohibited women in the Air Force and Navy from flying combat missions. But it's only a victory if you consider equal opportunity for bombing and strafing as an unadulterated feminist achievement.

> —ANNETTE FUENTES, author
> *The Nation*, October 1991

Close your eyes and they'll go away, her father says, or you're just imagining. And anyway, a woman's place is sleeping so she can wake up early with the tortilla star, the one that appears early just in time to rise and catch the hind legs hidden behind the sink, beneath the four-clawed tub, under the swollen floorboards nobody fixes in the corners of your eyes.

> —SANDRA CISNEROS, author
> "Alicia Who Sees Mice," *Barrios and Borderlands*

While the women I interviewed did collectively say, "In being Latina there are certain parts of me that need to change," at no point did any interviewee say, "I don't want to be a Latina." We have a bountiful cultural legacy—our history, language, music, art, folklore and food—a legacy we should always treasure. The aspects of our cultural traditions that serve a useful function should be retained. Those that are harmful and self-defeating should be examined closely, their adverse effects acknowledged, then discarded.

—BETTINA R. FLORES, author
Chiquita's Cocoon

The voices of feminists who consider combat inclusion a dubious advance have been muted. The sole debate has been between conservative types who think G.I. Jane will sabotage male bonding on the front lines and the equal rights advocates who argue that dropping all barriers to women in the military is not only fair, it contributes to military preparedness.

—ANNETTE FUENTES, author
The Nation, October 1991

In all the social classes, with the exception of those privileged with money, abnegation and work are the supreme feminine virtues. The spirit of sacrifice is a question of honor: the more they suffer for the family, the more pride they feel.

—ISABEL ALLENDE, author
Paula

The fog in my mirror
slowly unveils
a woman of bronze
earth and fire.

> —NAOMI QUIÑONEZ, author
> "Ánima," *In Other Words, Literature by
> Latinas of the United States*

Sex is still referred to by many Latinas as "you-know-what." Latinas are naïve about sex. They see it as a duty and, therefore, don't fake headaches too often. They view sex within marriage as okay because the church says it's okay, but sex before marriage makes them feel guilty.

> —BETTINA R. FLORES, author
> *Chiquita's Cocoon*

Hispanics are here for many different reasons. Many have been born here. Many were here before parts of this land came to be called the United States of America. Some came a lifetime ago. Some came yesterday. Some are arriving this very minute. Some dream of returning to where they came from. Some will. Women have made this place their home for good and are here to stay.

> —DOLORES PRIDA, author
> "The Show Does Go On," *Barrios and Borderlands*

From running households and families to running governments and corporations, women of all nationalities have certainly come a long way. But Hispanics are destined for an even greater future. A future that will call on their women's unique talents and abilities to carry for the American dream.

—ILEANA ROS-LEHTINEN, congresswoman
Rising Voices: Profiles in Leadership

Latinas in this country live in two worlds. People who don't know us may think we're fat. At home, we're called *bien cuidadas* (well cared for).

—CHRISTY HAUBEGGER, journalist
Essence, December 1994

Culturally, Latinas are expected to appear as if they have had few lovers and little knowledge of sex [New York clinical psychologist Sharlene] Bird said. If they ask assertively to have their sexual desires fulfilled, it sends a signal that the woman knows what she wants because she has experienced it before.

—INES PINTO ALICEA, journalist
Hispanic, January/February 1995

God has given his children equal talents and skills. Men and women complement each other. They should struggle side by side, not against each other. Women should have equal opportunities in politics as well as other fields.

—OLGA A. MENDEZ, state senator
Portraits

Healthy wolves and healthy women share certain psychic characteristics: keen sensing, playful spirit, and a heightened capacity for devotion. Wolves and women are relational by nature, inquiring, possessed of great endurance and strength. They are deeply intuitive, intensely concerned with their young, their mate, and their pack. They are experienced at adapting to constantly changing circumstances, they are fiercely stalwart and very brave.

—Clarissa Pinkola Estes, author
Women Who Run with the Wolves

WORK

I believe it is preferable to start off doing what one likes;
it's more difficult to change to what you want later.
>—María Conchita Alonso, actress, musician
>*Notable Hispanic American Women*

Look, look, here's my pay—a little dust. I can't even buy
a bottle of tequila.
>—Anthony Quinn, actor
>in *¡Viva Zapata!*

I am ready to work / all I ask is that I don't starve.
>—Jimmy Santiago Baca, author
>"Martin and Meditations on the South Valley," in
>volume 1 of *Hispanic Literature Criticism*

Work

I was invited to these [boards of directors for the Gillette Company and others] because of my understanding of economics and finance. Surprisingly, these appointments have established my status in the business community in ways that I had never achieved while I was a President's economic advisor. Executives immediately accept me on a different level because I'm a director of Fortune-500 companies.

—RITA RICARDO-CAMPBELL, senior fellow
Notable Hispanic American Women

WRITING/WRITERS

The way the Indians say "seeing" is how close you can come to the way things really are, the way a deer sees a rock, or the way a frog sees water; we call that "seeing." Every human being has that seeing in them, and someone who gets up and writes every day, all he or she is trying to do is to get close to his or her seeing capabilities.

—JIMMY SANTIAGO BACA, author
This Is About Vision

What I discovered is that I get to write. One of my jobs is to try to write these stories that I have. The two novels are my required thing so I can get into heaven. And the other things are extra.

It's like, wow, I'll just do these and I can die smilin'. Maybe I didn't do a lot of things right, but I did my job.

—DAGOBERTO GILB, author
Los Angeles Times Magazine, November 12, 1995

With a stub pencil I whittled sharp with my teeth, I propped a Red Chief notebook on my knees and wrote my first words. From that moment, a hunger for poetry possessed me.

—JIMMY SANTIAGO BACA, author
"Working in the Dark," in volume 1 of
Hispanic Literature Criticism

We know the stereotypes mediawise. But I take them and turn them around. It's like getting those demons out there and hitting them over the head. . . . Some Hispanics feel uncomfortable with what I'm doing. But we must bring out these characters in order to grow into other roles.

—JOHN LEGUIZAMO, actor
Hispanic, March 1992

[On his choice of characters:]
One editor said, "You know, they're all laborers or carpenters; they're all the same." Well, what's the difference between a banker and a receptionist? They're livin' in the same world. But a plumber and an electrician are not the same to me. And a mechanic is not the same as a carpenter. They just don't understand the class.

They don't expect Chicanos to be employed. They would look at my stories and say "Where are the cholos? Where are the curanderas? Where are the illegals? Where's the Chicano world? Where do you live?" Well, I'm in El Paso, and I'm tellin' you, this is how it is. They just didn't get it.

—DAGOBERTO GILB, author
Los Angeles Times Magazine, November 12, 1995

Autobiography creates its own time in rearranged memories. It orders random accidents into inevitability. I am able to reconstruct my life from birth, even before birth through inherited memories, and so to provide structure to what is shapeless, reason to anarchy—and the only meaning possible, a retrospective meaning, imposed; the only truth, one's own. That is, autobiography as novel.

—JOHN RECHY, author
Autobiography: A Novel

I never thought of lying in my writing. It would have been like hiding in the bathroom to read.

—DENISE CHÁVEZ, educator, performance artist
"Essay," in volume 1 of *Hispanic Literature Criticism*

If you are a Chicano writer you are bound to be in a constant struggle with yourself . . . That struggle is bound to be reflected in what we write. . . . The humiliation of having to be at the mercy of a crumb throwing society and even the acceptance of the role of adopting *nueva lengua* [a new language] and the idea of being on your own soil as a foreigner . . . all of these things have to be a set of themes with universal relationship, but with a very peculiar Chicano flavor.

—ABELARDO DELGADO, educator

Autobiography changes from moment to moment. It is not what happened but what is remembered. Its only sequence is that of memory. Alter the order of events and you change meaning.

—JOHN RECHY, author
Autobiography: A Novel

The political writer, then, is the ultimate optimist, believing people are capable of change and using words as one way to try and penetrate the privatism of our lives.

—CHERRÍE MORAGA and GLORIA ANZALDÚA, authors
This Bridge Called My Back

[On winning literary prizes:]
Before, you're writing and you feel like you're taking this leap. And you don't know if you're going to land or not; you're just in the air. And the awards came, and I landed in New York. Poof! It was sort of amazing. I was still in shock. You hit bottom, and the bottom turns into the top. It was definitely odd. New Mexico was not New York.

—DAGOBERTO GILB, author
Los Angeles Times Magazine, November 12, 1995

Some well-meaning people fret that Anglos may not receive a good impression of us. . . . If the Chicano writer tries to please that part of the Chicano public, he's in trouble. He's also in trouble if he tries to please any one special sector of the Chicano population. The writer should write the best he can; if he has weaknesses in his writing they'll show up soon enough. Chicano literature in all its phases and through all its genres may be a reflection of the Chicano and his life; however, what weaknesses there are must be leveled toward the authors who couldn't—or wouldn't—present the verities (as they honestly saw them) of all Chicanos: rural, urban, young, old, good, bad, sick, well, at home, at work, in love. . . .

—ROLANDO HINOJOSA-SMITH, author

My quest is to empower others as I empower myself through my comedy writing.

—RICK NAJERA, comedian

You've got to make fun of yourself in a comedy show. I'm not gonna portray all the Latinos as angelic, upwardly mobile, successful people, because that's boring and unreal. It's not representing what's going on.

—JOHN LEGUIZAMO, actor
Hispanic, May 1995

But what I used to love about construction that I hate about writing is that it was really about what you did and not how you yakked. Nothing to do with what you said; it was, "Did you build it? Did you build it on time?" I like that.

—DAGOBERTO GILB, author
Los Angeles Times Magazine,
November 12, 1995

But I don't know if literature was my destiny. I wanted to be a physicist, or a mathematician, and, before that, an archaeologist or anthropologist, and for a long time I wanted to be a painter. Because I was raised in a house full of writers and that wasn't for me. No, Ma'am. No thanks.

—LUISA VALENZUELA, author, educator
"Writing with the Body," *The Writer on Her Work*

Long before it was trendy and lucrative for Latino writers to weave tales of the Latin American experience for mainstream consumption, the masters like Nobel laureate Octavio Paz and Rudolfo Anaya imparted to the world the beauty and serenity and mysticism of Latin American people and their culture. These veteranos of the literary world, through their strong books of poetry and creative fiction, managed to not only define their own era but also to transcend the boundaries of time and inspire succeeding generations of Latino writers, both in Mexico and the United States.

> —RUBEN NAVARRETTE, JR., author
> *Roots of Greatness: The 1995 Mexican American Historical Calendar*

Picking out images from my soul's eye, fishing for the right words to recreate the images. Words are blades of grass pushing past the obstacles, sprouting on the page; the spirit of the words moving in the body is as concrete as flesh and as palpable; the hunger to create is as substantial as fingers and hand.

> —GLORIA ANZALDÚA, author
> "Tlilli, Tlapalli: The Path of the Red and Black Ink"

I'm like the least likely writer. Almost every writer I meet says they were writing their first story at six. Well, sorry, I didn't have any idea what a pen was then, you know? I wasn't into that. I wasn't one of these people who popped out of the womb and wrote about the womb experience.

> —DAGOBERTO GILB, author
> *Los Angeles Times Magazine*, November 12, 1995

I put my body where my words are.

The physical loss hasn't been as great for me as it has been for others. I haven't been tortured, beaten or persecuted. Knock on wood. I've been spared, perhaps because my statements aren't frontal; they are visions from the corner of my eye, oblique. I think we must continue writing about the horrors so that memory isn't lost and history won't repeat itself.

—LUISA VALENZUELA, author, educator

I had this myth in my head that you wrote s——, you sent it off to magazines, you got paid. And when you got paid, you tried to write more, and that's how it worked. But it isn't that way.

—DAGOBERTO GILB, author
Los Angeles Times Magazine, November 12, 1995

To write, to be a writer, I have to trust and believe in myself as a speaker, as a voice for the images. I have to believe that I can communicate with images and words and that I can do it well. A lack of belief in my creative self is a lack of belief in my total self and vice versa—I cannot separate my writing from any part of my life. It is all one.

—GLORIA ANZALDÚA, author
"Tlilli, Tlapalli: The Path of the Red and Black Ink"

APPENDIX

Maureen Leon Acosta is the director of Artistic Images and served as coproducer of *Expresiones Hispanas*, the 1988/89 Coors National Hispanic art exhibit and tour.

Francisco X. Alarcón, M.A., A.B.D., is an educator and poet with many publications to his credit. His awards include the 1993 American Book Award.

Ben Alicéa is associate director of Hispanic Programs for the Fund for Theological Education in New York City.

Ines Pinto Alicea is a writer for *Hispanic* magazine.

Adela Allen is a dean at the University of Arizona. She has been an educator and administrator there for over twenty years. She has been a board member on numerous academic and civic organizations, including the Tucson Symphony Society. In 1990 she won the Women on the Move Award.

Isabel Allende was a journalist for many years. *House of Spirits* was her first worldwide bestselling novel.

María Conchita Alonso began her career modeling and doing commercials and beauty pageants, becoming a popular and respected actress in American film as well as Venezuelan film and television. She is also a singer.

Linda Alvarado is president and owner of Alvarado Construction, Inc., based in Denver, Colorado. She is also a co-owner of the Colorado Rockies, a major league baseball team.

A. Alvarez is a writer/journalist whose work has appeared in publications such as *Encounter* and *Observer*.

Luis Alvarez is a much decorated experimental physicist. For many years he was the associate director of the Lawrence Berkeley Laboratories. In 1961 he was awarded the Einstein Medal. Twenty-five years later he was awarded the Nobel Prize in physics.

Originally from Cuba, **Mercedes Alvarez** is an advertising executive at the New York ad agency BBDO.

Rudolfo Anaya, M.A., is an author and educator whose work has been widely read, quoted, and anthologized. Anaya has been honored with a 1980 National Endowment for the Arts fellowship and a Kellogg Foundation Fellowship (1983–86).

Felix Angel is an architect, painter, writer, and lecturer. His comments on a national Hispanic art exhibit and tour appeared in *Expresiones Hispanas 88/89*, published by the Adolph Coors Company.

Lupe Anguiano lived as a Catholic nun for fifteen years before becoming an educator and community activist. *Hispanic Business Magazine* named her one of the hundred most influential Hispanics of the 1980s.

Gloria Anzaldúa is coauthor of *This Bridge Called My Back, Borderlands: The New Mestiza*, and most recently the children's story *The Ghost Woman's Gift*.

Paulette Atencio is a traditional storyteller and businesswoman who has also worked with the Artist in Residence Program in New Mexico. She is considering pursuing a career in politics.

Fransisco Avelar, known to listeners of his radio talk show as "Pancho del Rancho," is a teacher, low-key community activist, and radio personality in Los Angeles.

Jimmy Santiago Baca is a playwright, poet, and novelist. His works include *Black Mesa Poems* and an autobiography titled *In the Way of the Sun*. In 1989 he was awarded the National Hispanic Heritage Award.

Joan Baez is a singer/songwriter/activist who has been deeply involved in working for nonviolent change for causes such as human rights and peace. Her autobiography, *And a Voice to Sing With*, was published in 1987.

Kenneth B. Bedell is a computer specialist who is executive director of EPIC, Inc., in Dayton, Ohio. He is also an ordained minister. He is author of *The Role of Computers in Religious Education*.

Alfonso Bedoya was a character actor during the first half of the century. His most famous role was in John Huston's *The Treasure of the Sierra Madre*. Other films he starred in are: *Streets of Laredo*, *The Stranger Wore a Gun*, and *The Big Country*.

Robert Beltrán is an actor who has starred in many films including *Eating Raoul, Scenes from the Class Struggle in Beverly Hills*, and *Gaby, A True Story*.

Roxann Biggs-Dawson plays the half-Latina, half-Klingon B'Elanna Torres on the television series *Star Trek: Voyager*.

Rubén Blades, LL.M., actor, entertainer, composer, politician, and writer, began his career as an attorney. He has been honored in many capacities in the film and music industries, and has won two Grammy Awards. In 1993, he ran for president in Panama.

Giulio V. Blanc is an art historian, writer, consultant, and curator. His comments on a national Hispanic art exhibit and tour appeared in *Expresiones Hispanas 88/89*, published by the Adolph Coors Company.

Frank Bonilla, of El Centrode Estudios Puertorriqueños, is a political scientist who taught for many years at MIT, Stanford University, and City University of New York. Bonilla is best known for pioneering the field of Puerto Rican studies.

Humberto Calzada is a Cuban American artist. Recently a retrospective of his work was exhibited at the Bass Museum of Art.

Ana Castillo is a Chicago-born author who has published many literary works since her first, *Zero Makes Me Hungry*, in 1975.

Lorna Dee Cervantes is a poet and editor. She is best known for editing and publishing the literary review *Mango* and for her collection of poems, *Emplumada*.

César Chávez (1927–1993) was a volunteer organizer in Community Service Organizations before founding the National Farm Workers Association and the United Farm Workers of America. He was honored with the Aztec Eagle from the government of Mexico.

Denise Chávez, M.F.A., M.A., is an educator and performance writer whose work appears in many anthologies. She has done solo performances, readings, workshops, and lectures throughout the United States and Europe.

As executive vice president of the AFL-CIO, **Linda Chávez-Thompson** is involved in labor issues on the international scene.

Henry Cisneros, M.P.A., Ph.D., is secretary of the U.S. Department of Housing and Urban Development. He began his career as an educator in Texas. Cisneros was mayor of San Antonio for seven years.

Sandra Cisneros, M.F.A., is a writer and educator. Her work has been widely published in magazines and newspapers. Her collections of stories, poetry, and essays have received many literary awards.

Jesús Colón (1901–1974) came to the United States from his birthplace in Puerto Rico in 1918, when he was seventeen. A journalist, essayist, and fiction writer, Colon was the first to describe in English what life was like for the first Puerto Ricans to migrate to the United States.

Francisco Rodriguez Cruz was an editor of a communist party newspaper in Cuba during the 1970s. In 1980 he left Cuba and wound up in a tent camp at Fort Walton Beach, Florida. In a *Newsweek* interview that year he voiced his criticisms of the Castro government.

Rodolfo de la Garza, a professor at the University of Texas at Austin, is an educator, editor, and researcher whose career has been heavily invested in advising, consulting with, and participating in associations worldwide concerned with human rights, the social sciences, policy, and Hispanic and Latin American studies.

Abelardo Delgado is an educator who is active in the arts, literature, civil rights, justice, and equity activism. He is also a researcher and a columnist.

Porfirio Díaz (1830–1915) was President of Mexico from 1877–1880 and 1884–1911.

Miguel Domínguez, Ph.D., is a writer, educator, lecturer, curator, and member of the faculty of California State University.

Hector Elizondo is a professional actor and director with many film, stage, and television roles to his credit. He has performed in multiple Broadway productions and currently has a key role in the popular television series *Chicago Hope*.

Sergio Elizondo has been a professor of Spanish for most of his life, most recently at New Mexico State University. He has been awarded numerous grants and fellowships from organizations such as the NEA and the Ford Foundation.

Virgil Elizondo is a Roman Catholic priest and theologian. He has written widely on topics ranging from education to liberation theology.

Jaime Escalante, the renowned educator whose life was honored in the 1987 film *Stand and Deliver*, was born in Bolivia and completed his education in Los Angeles. He has received honors for teaching mathematics and is the founder of the Escalante Mathematics Program.

Gloria Estefan is a popular singer, songwriter, and performer who first became known as a member of the Miami Sound Machine in the 1970s and is now a famous solo artist. She has received many music industry awards and has a star on the Hollywood Walk of Fame.

Clarissa Pinkola Estes, writer, Jungian analyst, and specialist in cross-cultural mythology, is the author of several books, including *Women Who Run with the Wolves*.

Sandra Maria Esteves, born in the South Bronx, writes, performs, directs, and produces. A visual artist, she is a strong supporter of other artists' work. The excerpts from her work are found in *Puerto Rican Writers at Home in the USA*, an anthology edited by Faythe Turner.

Alfredo Estrada is editor and publisher of *Hispanic* magazine.

José Ferrer is an actor and director with a long career in the film business. His films include *Joan of Arc*, *Caine Mutiny*, and *Lawrence of Arabia*. In 1950 he won an Academy Award for Best Actor for his work in *Cyrano*.

Pablo Figueroa is author of *Enrique* and a history of Hispanic theater in New York. He's also an independent filmmaker.

Bettina R. Flores is the author of *Chiquita's Cocoon, Chiquita's Diary, Teacher Resource for Chiquita's Diary*, and *Chiquita's Challenge Workbook*. Ms. Flores lectures, writes a syndicated column, and leads Chiquita's Challenge Seminars nationally. She is also the creator of Chiquita Bonita Dolls, and stars in the television series *Chiquita's Cocoon*, which she co-produces. Ms. Flores is referred to as the "Betty Friedan" for the Latina woman.

Evelína Freelandes is an actress whose views were published in an Internet article in 1995.

Kid Frost is a rap recording artist with Virgin Records. His albums include *Hispanic Causing Panic* and *East Side Story*.

Annette Fuentes is a coauthor with Barbara Ehrenreich of *Women in the Global Factory*.

Carlos Fuentes, professor of Latin American Studies at Harvard University, is widely published in many genres. His novels include *The Death of Artemio Cruz* and *The Campaign*, and *Myself and Others* is a collection of his essays. Many of the Fuentes quotes in this volume can be found in *The Graywolf Annual Five: Multi-Cultural Literacy*.

Daisy Fuentes is a physical-fitness educator. Her exercise video is titled *Daisy Fuentes—Totally Fit!*

Larry Gabriel is an actor. His credits include the film *Cave Girl*.

Carlos Gaivar, a veteran broadcast journalist/producer, has worked in numerous radio and television venues. He produced the award-winning documentary series *¡Viva Latino!*, chairs the National Federation of Hispanics in Communications, and is now with KNX, Los Angeles.

Nely Galán, a television producer, broke into the world of television early as host of syndicated talk shows, including *Bravo*, and now owns a production company.

Appendix

Andy García is a film actor who has starred in Brian De Palma's *The Untouchables* and *The Godfather III*, among others.

Robert García has worked in radio for over twenty years. He is currently executive producer of CBS Radio.

Alex García-Rivera, formerly a Lutheran pastor, now works within the Catholic Church.

Beatriz de la Garza is president of the board of trustees of Austin, Texas. Her collection of short stories was published in 1994. It is titled *The Candy Vendor's Boy and Other Stories*.

Dagoberto Gilb is a carpenter and writer. He has been a writer in residence at a number of universities, including the University of Texas at Austin. He was the winner of the PEN/Hemingway Foundation award in 1994 for his collections of stories.

Vernon Louis "Lefty" Gomez was a pitcher and is a member of the major league baseball Hall of Fame. Over a career spanning fourteen seasons, he played in seven straight All-Star games and won twenty games a season four times. He still holds the best win-loss record for World Series play: 6–0.

A visual artist and performance artist originally from Mexico, **Guillermo Gómez-Peña** may be best known to some audiences in the United States for his tours in highly stylized and satiric performances in which he and artist Coco Fusco played caged primitive Amerindians on display.

Henry González is a U.S. Congressman for the state of Texas. Prior to becoming a congressman he served the people of

Texas as a city councilman in San Antonio and as a state senator.

Justo L. González, S.T.B., S.T.M., M.A., Ph.D., is a writer heavily involved with education and theology, editor for *Apuntes*, director of the Hispanic Summer Program of the Fund for Theological Education, and editor of the *Comentario Biblico Hispanoamericano*.

Rudolfo "Corky" González was a Presbyterian leader during the Brown Power movement of the 1960s. His epic poem *Yo Soy Joaquin*, published in pamphlet form in 1964 and passed from hand to hand at the grassroots level, was a key motivator of the movement.

Carlos V. Grijalva, Jr., M.A., Ph.D., is a psychologist on the faculty of the University of California at Los Angeles. He has contributed to many scholarly publications on psychology, neuroscience, and medicine.

Jose Angel Gutierrez is a judge for the city of Dallas. Before becoming a judge he was instrumental in organizing many important Hispanic organizations. He is a cofounder of the La Raza Unida Party, the Mexican American Unity Council, and the Mexican American Youth Organization.

Christy Haubegger is an attorney. She is coauthor of *Cutting Edge Cases in the Legal Environment of Business*.

David Hayes-Bautista is an associate editor at Pacific News Service. He is also director of the Center for the Study of Latino Health at UCLA.

Guillermo E. Hernández is associate professor of Spanish at the University of California, Los Angeles. His book *Chicano*

Appendix

Satire: A Study in Literary Culture is published by the University of Texas Press.

Sandra Hernández is a costume designer. Her credits include the films *Money Train*, *Malcolm X*, and *Clockers*.

Tish Hinojosa is a guitarist and recording artist. She has made a number of recordings in both English and Spanish. Her albums include *Culture Swing*, *Frontejas*, and *Destiny's Gate*.

Rolando Hinojosa-Smith, Ph.D., is an author and educator in Texas. His novels, articles, and essays have been widely published, here and abroad.

Mark Holston is a journalist who writes about music for *Hispanic* magazine and *Americas*.

Dolores Huerta is the most renowned Chicana labor leader in the United States. With César Chávez she cofounded the United Farm Workers union. She is sometimes referred to as Dolores "Huelga" (strike).

Marta Istomin is president of the Manhattan School of Music in New York. Prior to her present position she was the artistic director at the Kennedy Center for the Performing Arts in Washington, D.C. She was wife to the musician Pablo Casals for seventeen years until his death in 1973.

Mari-Luci Jaramillo is an educator and was U.S. Ambassador to Honduras during the administration of President Jimmy Carter. She is now assistant vice president for Educational Testing Services, a major nonprofit testing corporation.

Luis Jiménez is a sculptor who is famous for his works of resin epoxy and fiberglass. Over the years he has also worked with charcoal pencil. His best-known series of drawings is titled *Indian to Rockets*. The series is based on post office murals of the Southwest.

Raúl Julia (1940–1995) was a professional actor celebrated worldwide for his roles in films (*The Eyes of Laura Mars*, *Kiss of the Spider Woman*, *Havana*), stage performances, and television appearances. He was active in Hispanic organizations and in Project Hunger.

Elena Kellner is an entertainment columnist for the *Los Angeles Times*.

Edith LaFontaine is the editor of *El Interprete*, the Spanish-language magazine of the United Methodist Church.

Fernando Lamas has played in a number of television series and TV movies. The most popular shows he worked on were *Medical Center* and *The Rookies*. Both series aired during the 1970s. Billy Crystal has immortalized him by popularizing his line, "You Look Maaaaarvelous!"

Gustavo LeClerc, co-founder of *ADOBE L.A.* (Architects and Designers Opening the Border Edge of L.A.) and director of Public Art at SPARC (Social and Public Art Resource Center), is an architect and artist who documents the cultural landscape of Los Angeles as it is influenced by Latino contributions such as murals, garden shrines, and other public art.

Born in Colombia, **John Leguizamo** is a comedian, actor, and performance artist. He has made a successful career in Hollywood as a writer and actor, with roles in films such as *Die Hard 2* and *Hanging with the Homeboys*.

Appendix

Alberto Lopez is director of the Hispanic marketing division at Burrell Public Relations in Chicago. He is also the publisher of *Lowrider Magazine*.

Lalo Lopez is a writer and journalist. He writes a regular column for the *LA Weekly*.

M.C. GeeGee is a contemporary Christian rap recording artist. His most recent release is *And Now the Mission Continues*.

Luis Madrigal is the executive director of the Hispanic Association of Bilingual-Bicultural Ministries.

Miguel O. Martinez is an artist. His work has been exhibited in New Mexico and Arizona.

Rubén Martíncz is an author and journalist. During his career he has worked as a freelance journalist, a staff writer for the Los Angeles alternative paper *LA Weekly*, and as cohost of the public television program *Life and Times* on KCET in Los Angeles. His current project is a book about Mexico in the 1990s.

Antonio Mejías-Rentas is a columnist and editor for *La Opinion*, the newspaper in Los Angeles.

Mello Man Ace is a rap recording artist. His most recent release is *Can't Stop Moving*.

Olga Mendez has been a New York state senator for almost twenty years. She received her Ph.D. from Yeshiva University and taught in the state university system in New York before running for office.

Ralph Mercado is a music-industry producer, promoter, and executive. He has promoted Tito Puente, Rubén Blades, Celia Cruz, and others, and has been honored for his efforts by awards such as New York City mayor David Dinkins's proclamation during Salsa Week Festival in 1991.

Jesse Miranda is the associate dean of the Haggard School of Theology at Azusa Pacific University in Southern California.

Allessandra Moctezuma, Principal architect with *ADOBE L.A.* (Architects and Designers Opening the Border Edge of L.A.), is a multidisciplinary artist and architect participating with other artists and architects in expressing Latino presence in Los Angeles' visual identity.

Nicholasa Mohr is one of the few Latinas who has managed to get her work published by New York publishers. She has won many awards for her novels and stories for adults and children.

Gloria Molina has collected over her career a number of firsts. She was the first Chicana elected to the California State Assembly, first Chicana elected to the Los Angeles City Council, and the first Chicana elected to the Los Angeles County Board of Supervisors—her present position.

Ricardo Montalbán is a Mexican-born actor best known for his role in the long-running television show *Fantasy Island*. He has also starred in numerous films such as *Star Trek II: The Wrath of Khan* and earlier *Escape from the Planet of the Apes*.

Jose Montes de Oca is an author who was born near the end of the nineteenth century. He authored many books including *Tasca*, *Manchas de Color*, and *A Traves de la Meloncolia*, *Cuentes*.

Pat Mora is a poet, educator, and author of a number of children's books. She has published three books of poems, *Chants*, *Borders*, and *Communion*. Her best-known children's books are *A Birthday Basket for Tia* and *Pablo's Tree*.

Cherríe Moraga is one of the most prominent lesbian Chicana writers in the United States. She has edited and authored a number of essay anthologies and plays. Her most celebrated work is *This Bridge Called My Back: Writings by Radical Women of Color*, which she edited with Gloria Anzaldúa.

Aurora Levins Morales has lived in Puerto Rico; New York City; Rochester, New York; Ann Arbor, Michigan; and Chicago. She writes poetry, nonfiction, and fiction, has worked in radio and theater, and is the coauthor of *Getting Home Alive*, a collection of poetry and prose, with her mother, Rosario Morales.

Esai Morales is a film actor who has played alongside Sean Penn, Jim Belushi, and Madonna. He has worked on *Bad Boys*, *Bloodhounds of Broadway*, and *The Principal*. One of his best performances can be seen in *La Bamba*.

Rosario Morales is a poet and essayist. Her work "I Am What I Am" can be found anthologized in many literature collections.

Antonio Moreno was a film star in the first half of the century. He worked in many films, opposite such stars as Greta Garbo and Gloria Swanson. His typical role was that of a Latin lover.

Rita Moreno is the only entertainer in the world to have received all four of entertainment's most prestigious awards: an Emmy, a Grammy, an Oscar, and a Tony. She also has a star on the Hollywood Walk of Fame.

Rick Najera is a comedy writer and stage and television performer, director, and producer, who has worked on programs such as *In Living Color*, *Culture Clash*, and *The Robert Townsend Show*. He also tours with his one-man show, *The Pain of the Macho*.

Gregory Nava is a film director. His film *El Norte*, released in 1984, was a poignant story about a brother and sister's escape from the social turmoil racking their South American homeland, and their travails as they make their way north to the United States.

Ruben Navarrette, Jr., is author of *A Darker Shade of Crimson: Odyssey of a Harvard Chicano*. He edits the newsletter "Reconciliation."

Alex Nogales is a board member and currently serves as an officer of the National Hispanic Media Coalition.

Ramón Novarro was a popular actor in the first half of the century. He played alongside Greta Garbo in *Mata Hari* and starred in many other films. He is best known for the role Ben-Hur in the silent film version of *Ben-Hur*.

Antonía Novello, M.D., M.P.H., former U.S. Surgeon General, was the first Hispanic and first woman to hold that position. Dr. Novello has been widely honored for her contributions in medicine, specifically in pediatrics, public health, and nephrology.

Jaime Oaxaca, member of the National Science Foundation Board, among others, is a past vice president of the Northrop Corporation, where he began his career as an engineer.

Adriana C. Ocampo is a planetary geologist with NASA at Jet Propulsion Labs. Born in Colombia and educated in Los Angeles, Ms. Ocampo was involved with Project Galileo to Jupiter and the Mars Observor mission.

Father Luis Olivares (1934–1993), pastor of Our Lady Queen of Angels Roman Catholic Church in Los Angeles until his death, was an advocate of the poor and the undocumented. Padre Olivares died of AIDS contracted from a blood transfusion during a visit to El Salvador.

Edward James Olmos is an actor, producer, and director in the film industry. His career was launched by his starring role in both the stage and screen version of *Zoot Suit*. Since then he has starred in such films as *Stand and Deliver* and *Blade Runner*. He most recently directed the film *American Me*.

Katherine Ortega became the first female president of a California bank when she took the position at Santa Ana State Bank in 1975. Eight years later she attained even greater heights by becoming Treasurer of the United States during Ronald Reagan's administration.

Dyana Ortelli is a television and film star. She has worked on such films as *La Bamba, Born in East L.A.*, and *American Me*.

Américo Paredes taught anthropology and folklore at the University of Texas for many years. He is one of the most distinguished scholars of folklore in the United States. In 1986 he won the prestigious Charles Frankel award from the NEA.

In 1991 the Mexican government bestowed upon him their most coveted award, the Aguila Azteca medal.

Elizabeth Peña has performed in many movies, including *La Bamba*, **batteries not included*, and *Down and Out in Beverly Hills*, as well as on television and in theater.

Federico Peña, J.D., is secretary of the U.S. Department of Transportation. He began his career as an attorney and then moved into politics as a member of the Colorado General Assembly and as mayor of Denver. He was honored as Colorado's Outstanding House Democratic Legislator in 1981.

Hugo Pineda is an author. His latest work was published in 1994 in Chile. It is titled *El Intruso del Sur*.

Merrihelen Ponce is an author and scholar. She has taught Chicano studies at the Los Angeles and Santa Barbara campuses of the University of California. Her most recent works are *Hoyt Street*, an autobiography, and *The Wedding*, a work of fiction.

Estela Portillo Trambley is an educator and writer who lives in El Paso, Texas. Her novels have won awards, and she also writes poetry and for the theater. Her early work was published in *El Grito*, the first journal associated with the Chicano movement.

Joanne Pottlitzer compiled a study for the Ford Foundation on Hispanic theater in America called *Hispanic Theater in the United States and Puerto Rico*.

Dolores Prida was born in Cuba and fled with thousands of other Cubans after Fidel Castro came to power. She is a playwright currently working in New York. She has written many plays, most notably *Beautiful Senoritas* and *Coser y Cantar*.

Tito Puente (El Rey) is a musician and well-known orchestra leader who has recorded with jazz greats including Lionel Hampton and Dizzie Gillespie. He has appeared in movies such as *Radio Days* and *The Mambo Kings*, and has a star on the Hollywood Walk of Fame.

Anthony Quinn has appeared in over 180 films and won two Oscars. He is one of the few Hispanic actors who has been able to play non-Hispanic roles regularly. He is remembered for his roles in such film greats as: *The Hunchback of Notre Dame*, *Lawrence of Arabia*, *The Greek Tycoon*, and *Zorba the Greek*.

Naomi Quiñonez, M.A., Ph.D., is a published poet, educator, and community relations expert whose work has been honored by grants from the National Endowment for the Arts and the California Arts Council. She received the American Book Award from the Before Columbus Foundation in 1990.

John Rechy is a novelist and screenwriter whose work has been translated into more than a dozen languages. His books include *The Miraculous Day of Amalia Gómez*, *City of Night*, *Marilyn*, and *Bodies and Souls*. Rechy has been a mentor, teacher, and inspiration to dozens of L.A. writers.

Esther Rentería is on the board of the Hispanic Public Relations Association in Los Angeles and is a founding member and immediate past chairwoman of the board of the National Hispanic Media Coalition.

Luis Reyes is a publicist working in Hollywood, California.

Rita Ricardo-Campbell, senior fellow at the Hoover Institution, Stanford University, has served on several presidents' advisory committees as well as on corporate boards.

Dennis Mario Rivera has been president of the National Health and Human Services Employees Union since 1989.

Tomás Rivera was an author and university administrator. His novel . . . *y no se lo trago la tierra* won the very first Premio Quinto Sol award given to outstanding Chicano literature. This novel, which draws upon his own early life as a migrant worker, is still one of the best-selling Chicano novels.

ChiChi Rodriguez was born in Puerto Rico and rose to golf stardom beginning as a caddy. His flamboyant style has won him the affection of millions of golf fans. His talent as a golfer has won him millions of dollars on both the PGA tour and the Senior PGA tour.

Richard Rodriguez is an editor at the Pacific News Service. He is an acclaimed writer and journalist. His first book, *Hunger of Memory*, tells of his education being raised as Mexican and American. His essays can be seen on *The NewsHour with Jim Lehrer* on PBS.

Roberto Rodriguez is a filmmaker whose films include *El Mariachi*, *Desperado*, and *From Dusk Til Dawn*.

Ileana Ros-Lehtinen is a U.S. Congresswoman representing the state of Florida. Prior to entering the halls of Congress, she represented Floridians at the state level. She was the first Hispanic woman to be elected to office in both cases.

Tony Sabournin is director of press and publicity for Sony Discos, Inc., in Miami, Florida.

Appendix

Rubén Salazar was a popular television reporter who worked in Los Angeles. He died at the hands of the Los Angeles police during the Chicano Moratorium in August 1970. It is claimed that he was killed purposely for his reports critical of the LAPD's relationship with the Mexican American community in Los Angeles.

Ramona Salgado is a family counselor and professor at City University of New York. She has taught there for over twenty-five years.

Armando Sanchez is the founder of the Latino Scholastic Achievement Corporation. In addition to his efforts in public service, Sanchez has long devoted himself to education as a high school teacher in Los Angeles.

Ricardo Sánchez, Ph.D., is a writer, performer, and educator who has received many honors and awards, including Poet in Residency for the National Endowment for the Arts in 1975–76. Formerly a columnist and a bookstore owner, he continues to teach English and comparative cultures.

Moises Sandoval has been an editor at *Maryknoll Magazine* for a quarter century. He has won awards from both the Ford Foundation and the Alicia Patterson Foundation.

Jon Secada is a recording artist. His recordings include *Amor* and *Si Te Vas*. On Frank Sinatra's recording *Duet II*, Secada sang a duet with Mr. Sinatra.

José Luis Sedano represents the MALDEF (Mexican American Legal Defense and Education Foundation) Leadership Alumni Association on the National Hispanic Media Coalition Board, and is a cofounder and board member of the National Hispanic Media Coalition, an organization dedicated to advancing the employment of Hispanic Americans in all fields of media and the entertainment industry.

Martin Sheen (Ramón Estévez) is a popular film actor and father to two sons who are also actors. His best work can be seen in *The Execution of Private Slovik*, *Badlands*, and the epic Francis Ford Coppola film *Apocalypse Now*.

António Stevens-Arroyo, M.A., Ph.D., is a educator who has worked in research and policy fields, directed Puerto Rican studies programs, and been involved in analysis and activism in religion and theological studies, with awards such as National Endowment for the Humanities.

Reies Lopez Tijerina was a member of the organization Alianza in New Mexico during the 1970s. He was imprisoned in that state for demanding that the state and federal government return New Mexican land to the Indians and Spanish Americans.

Joseph Tovares is a video and television producer. He coproduced the television series *Americas* in 1993 and was the series editor of the television special *Chicago 1968*.

Luis M. Valdez is a producer, writer, theater director, and educator who holds several honorary doctorates. Founder and artistic director of El Teatro Campesino, he directed and wrote the screenplays for *Zoot Suit*, *La Bamba*, and *The Cisco Kid* and was the screenwriter for *Bandido*.

Luisa Valenzuela first came to the United States through the International Writers Workshop at the University of Iowa in 1969. She has lived here and abroad ever since, teaching and writing novels, short stories, and plays. Valenzuela received a Guggenheim Fellowship in 1983.

Ed Vega is one of the most prolific Hispanic writers living. His novel *The Comeback* tells the surreal story of a half-Puerto Rican, half-Eskimo hockey player caught up in a revolutionary movement. His most recent work is *Casualty Report*.

Victor Villaseñor is one of the most widely read Mexican-American novelists. His works include *Rain of Gold*.

Raúl Yzaguirre is the president of the National Council of La Raza, and has served in the U.S. Office of Economic Opportunity and in the Office of the President of the United States, among others. He is the founder of the Center for Community Change and was executive director from 1969 to 1973.

Bernice Zamora is a Chicana poet whose collection of poetry, *Restless Serpents*, is one of the seminal works of Chicana poetry.

Del Zamora is an actor. Some of the films he has worked on are: *Repo Man*, *Born in East L.A.*, *Robocop*, and the made-for-television movie *In the Line of Duty: The Price of Vengeance*.

Rudy Zea is a Colombian psychologist who practices family therapy in Maryland.

Ⓟ **PLUME**  **MERIDIAN**

"QUOTE, UNQUOTE"—MEMORABLE WORDS FOR READERS, WRITERS, SPEAKERS

☐ **THE NEW QUOTABLE WOMAN** *The Definite Treasury of Notable Words By Women from Eve to the Present* **Elaine Partnow, Editor.** Over 15,000 quotes from more than 2,500 women, including . . . history's most famous—and infamous women. . . . A definitive treasury of both familiar and unexpected quotations by women on nearly every subject imaginable from friendship, love, politics, religion, education, the arts and women's role in society. . . . This provocative volume is an inspiring testament to the power of women. (010993—$15.00)

☐ **A DICTIONARY OF QUOTATIONS FROM SHAKESPEARE** *A Topical Guide to Over 3,000 Great Passages from the Plays, Sonnets, and Narrative Poems.* **Selected by Margaret Miner and Hugh Rawson.** Filled with familiar treasures and unexpected delights, this superb collection offers exquisitely stated, witty, and profound commentary on life as we still experience it today, on our emotions and needs, and on both the grandeur and the foolishness of the human condition. An essential reference for readers, writers, students, and language lovers. (011272—$14.95)

☐ **THE FIRE IN OUR SOULS** *Quotations of Wisdom and Inspiration by Latino Americans* **by Rosie Gonzalez. Foreword by Edward James Olmos.** This unique collection pays tribute to the culture and experience of America's 26 million Latinos with hundreds of quotes from artists, political leaders, writers, and activists. Divided into topics, this poignant book offers reflections by such well-known figures as Andy Garcia, Sandra Cisneros, Lefty Gomez, César Chávez, and many more. (276845—$10.95)

Prices slightly higher in Canada.

Visa and Mastercard holders can order Plume, Meridian, and Dutton books by calling
1-800-253-6476.
They are also available at your local bookstore. Allow 4-6 weeks for delivery.
This offer is subject to change without notice.

Ⓟ **PLUME**

CAN I QUOTE YOU?

☐ **THE WIT AND WISDOM OF JOHN F. KENNEDY** *An A-to-Z Compendium of Quotations.* **Edited by Alex Ayres.** This volume brings together the most memorable quotations from America's youngest President's written and spoken words, arranged alphabetically by topic. Also included are his Inaugural Address, the text of the speech he was to give in Dallas on the day of his assassination, along with his other history-making speeches. (011396—$11.95)

☐ **THE WIT AND WISDOM OF ELEANOR ROOSEVELT** *An A-to-Z Compendium of Quotations.* **Edited by Alex Ayres.** Eleanor Roosevelt is one of our century's most inspiring figures. In this volume are memorable quotations from her books, newspaper columns, and speeches, arranged alphabetically by subject, and enriched by information about her life. They reflect the vast scope of her interests, the nobility of her sympathies, the courage of her convictions, and the keen intelligence she brought to bear on the thorniest issues of our age. (011388—$10.95)

☐ **THE WIT AND WISDOM OF ABRAHAM LINCOLN** *An A-Z Compendium of Quotes from the Most Eloquent of American Presidents.* **Edited by Alex Ayres.** Enlightening and inspiring, this unique collection gathers the best, funniest, most profound sayings of this most quotable of Chief Executives. (010896—$10.95)

☐ **THE WIT AND WISDOM OF MARK TWAIN. Edited by Alex Ayres.** Arranged alphabetically by topic, this wonderful, browsable collection has gathered the best of Twain, his most trenchant—or most outrageous—quips, sayings, one-liners, and humor—not only from his beloved novels, but from his speeches, letters, and conversations. (010586—$10.95)

Prices slightly higher in Canada.

Visa and Mastercard holders can order Plume, Meridian, and Dutton books by calling
1-800-253-6476.
They are available at your local bookstore. Allow 4-6 weeks for delivery.
This offer is subject to change without notice.

DUTTON

 PLUME

QUOTABLES

☐ **LIFE LESSONS FROM THE BRADY'S** *Far-out Advice From America's Grooviest TV Family.* **Unauthorized and Hilarious by Anthony Rubino, Jr.** Stop teeter-tottering around, drop your "Kitty Karry-All" and pick up this all-together, far-out collection of life lessons from the family that can solve any problem in less than a half-hour. It's a blast from the past that will have you rapping about your favorite episodes and digging the Bradys' insightful wisdom. (274419—$6.95)

☐ **LEO ROSTEN'S CARNIVAL OF WIT** *From Aristotle to Woody Allen.* **Edited by Leo Rosten.** Here is a connoisseur's alphabetically arranged collection of more than 5,000 of the funniest things people have said and written over the centuries and over the world. Whether you're looking for a wry grin, a silent chuckle, or a belly laugh, this classic collection will light up you mind, warm up your heart, and brighten up your life. (270995—$14.95)

☐ **ON THE NIGHT THE HOGS ATE WILLIE** *And Other Quotations on All Things Southern* **by Barbara Binswanger and Jim Charlton.** There's never been a collection of quotes that captures the delightful ambiguities of Dixieland—until this wonderful compendium of provocative, serious, seriously funny observations on all things Southern. Here are almost 800 inimitable examples of wit and wisdom about everything from Old Man River to Grand Ole Opry, from Graceland to a town called Hope, from Tara to Tobacco Road. (937625—$17.95)

☐ **THE PORTABLE CURMUDGEON. Compiled and Edited by Jon Winokur.** More than 1000 outrageously irreverent quotations, anecdotes, and interviews on a vast array of subjects, from an illustrious list of world-class grouches. (266688—$9.95)

Prices slightly higher in Canada.

Visa and Mastercard holders can order Plume, Meridian, and Dutton books by calling
1-800-253-6476.
They are also available at your local bookstore. Allow 4-6 weeks for delivery.
This offer is subject to change without notice.

PLUME   **DUTTON**    **MERIDIAN**

WORDS TO THE WISE

☐ **NO CHAIRS MAKE FOR SHORT MEETINGS** *And Other Business Maxims from Dad* **by Richard Rybolt.** Over 150 of the author's timeless ideas and adages teach an effective business philosophy that every working person, from laborer to company president, can instantly understand and implement. From specific advice on beating out the competition to keeping one's priorities straight, this charming book is proof that nice guys can finish first. (271940—$6.95)

☐ **FATHERS. Compiled and Edited by Jon Winokur.** Bitter or sweet, sentimental and barbed—this compendium of anecdotes, quips, and essays celebrates famous names and ordinary folks. Candice Bergen, Arthur Ashe, Alice Walker, Thurgood Marshall, and more than 200 others remember their fathers to offer moving and humorous testimony to the enduring legacy of fathers. (272076—$9.95)

☐ **THE WIT AND WISDOM OF WILL ROGERS. Edited by Alex Ayres.** An entertaining book from a national resource whose wit and wisdom are as vital and valid today as when he delivered them. Filled with such memorable quotes as (on stocks): "Don't gamble; take all your savings and buy some good stock, then hold it till it goes up, then sell it. If it don't go up, don't buy it." (011159—$11.95)

Prices slightly higher in Canada.

Visa and Mastercard holders can order Plume, Meridian, and Dutton books by calling
1-800-253-6476.
They are also available at your local bookstore. Allow 4-6 weeks for delivery.
This offer is subject to change without notice.